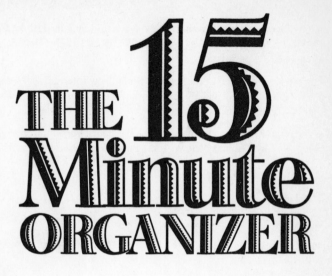

THE 15 Minute ORGANIZER

Emilie Barnes

HARVEST HOUSE PUBLISHERS
Eugene, Oregon 97402

The material in this book has appeared in somewhat similar form in previous issues of *Virtue* magazine.

THE 15-MINUTE ORGANIZER

Copyright © 1991 by Harvest House Publishers
Eugene, Oregon 97402

Library of Congress Cataloging-in-Publication Data

Barnes, Emilie.
    The fifteen minute organizer / by Emilie Barnes.
    ISBN 0-89081-857-6
      1. Time management—Religious aspects—Christianity.   2. Women—Conduct of life.   3. Women—Religious life.   4. Christian life—1960-
  I. Title. II. Title: 15 minute organizer.
  BV4598.5B37   1991   90-20593
  640′.43—dc20   CIP

Printed in the United States of America.

Dedication

This book is dedicated to the many readers of my series article, "The Sage Hen," that has appeared in *Virtue* magazine since 1983.

Over the years you have been a real encouragement to me with your many cards and letters. You have been a real inspiration to me by letting me know what information women want in order to make their lives more manageable.

Many of you are hustled, hassled, and hurried, and this book is written just for you. May your 15 minutes of reading give you many hours of peace.

I truly thank you for giving me the encouragement and motivation to address the topics of home and personal organization. You have truly helped me, and I thank you for that.

Emilie Barnes

Contents

FINANCES

HOLIDAY

FOODS AND KITCHEN

ORGANIZATION

AUTOMOBILE

TIME FOR YOU

MISCELLANEOUS

Introduction

We live in a very hurried-up society. There is not enough time for love, marriage, children, vacations, listening to music, and reading a good book. Our television programming has to fit into a 30-minute time allotment; a TV character must go from birth to death within this time period!

In a sense we are all in a hurry to get life over with. We demand instant cures, fast-food eating, and fast-forward buttons on our VCR's.

This book has been adapted from the last seven years of my articles of "The Sage Hen" in *Virtue* magazine for the person who needs to fit a lot of things into a short period of time. The purpose of this book is to provide brief but effective solutions to many of our basic organizational questions. Each chapter is short and to the point, especially designed for the person who has limited time to read a book.

This book can be read cover to cover, or else it can be used as a reference book to be placed on your bookshelf, to be read when you are looking for the answer to a particular question.

I have developed each chapter out of my own needs. Over the years I have met many people at our seminars who have had the same organizational needs that I have solved in my own life. I think you will find these ideas to be an encouragement to you as you become frustrated and cry out, "I can't seem to get organized, and my world is falling apart!"

Our motto is: "Fifteen minutes a day and you're on your way to having more hours in your day!" Make this a battle cry in your home, and you'll see how well it works!

Getting Started

Goal Setting Made Easy

While they are still talking to me about their needs, I will go ahead and answer their prayers!
—Isaiah 65:24

*D*O YOU WANT to set goals but shy away from it because of past failures in following through with your goals, or just because you don't know how to set a goal?

With a little information you can learn how to properly set goals for your life. Proverbs 29:18 states that if we have no vision we will perish. You are either moving ahead or falling back; there is no middle ground. I label the meaning of a goal as *a dream with a deadline*. Sometimes our goals aren't very achievable because they aren't very measurable. We have goals such as "I want to lose weight," "I want to eat better," "I want to be a better wife," or "I want to be more spiritual." These are all good desires, but we can't measure them and they don't have any deadlines.

There are two very important parts to goal-setting. Goals must include:

- A statement of quantity (how much)
- A date to complete (deadline)

A proper statement of a goal would be "I would like to lose 15 pounds by March 15." This way I can determine whether I have reached my goal. But remember that goals aren't cast in concrete; they just point you in the right direction. You can always rewrite, restate, or even cancel any goal.

As the beginning point of goal-setting, I recommend that you write down your goals that you want to accomplish within the next 90 days. As you get proficient in 90 days go out to six months, then nine months, then one year. Bite off little pieces at first; don't choke on a mouthful.

You might ask the same questions that a lot of people ask who come to my seminars: For what areas of my life should I write goals? In my own goal-setting I try to concentrate on eight areas:

1. Physical goals
2. Marriage/family goals
3. Financial goals
4. Professional goals
5. Mental goals
6. Social goals
7. Community support goals
8 Spiritual goals

These are not listed in any special priority, but are randomly listed for consideration when I want to get a grip on my life. An example of a 90-day goal for each of these areas would be:

1. I want to do 50 sit-ups by March 1.
2. I want to plan a 25th wedding anniversary party for my parents by April 15.
3. I want to save $250.00 by February 28.
4. I plan to enroll in an accounting class at the community college by April 2.
5. I plan to memorize the state capitals by May 5.
6. I plan on inviting the Merrihews, Planchons, and Hendricksens to a roller skating party on March 26.
7. I will take the Red Cross fliers to my neighbors on February 14.
8. I plan to read the Gospels of the New Testament by April 1.

Notice that each goal states a quantity and gives a date for completion. Each goal is measurable. As you complete each goal, take a pen and draw a line through that goal. This action will make you feel good about goal-setting.

As you complete each goal, you might want to write a new goal to take its place for the next 90 days.

Establishing Daily Priorities

Never be lazy in your work, but
serve the Lord enthusiastically.

—*Romans 12:11*

I'VE GOT so many things to do today that I don't know where to begin!" Is that how you feel on many days? This statement is shared by many people because they have never learned to establish daily priorities.

This article will give you tools for solving the dilemma "what do I do next?" Tools needed for this exercise are:

- Sheet of paper
- 3 x 5 cards
- Pen or pencil

Label your sheet of paper "TO DO" and list all the things you have been requested to do for today. When you are requested to do something, you need to ask yourself two basic questions:

1. Do I want to take advantage of this opportunity?
2. Shall I take part in this particular activity?

After asking the two questions you may answer in one of three ways:

Yes   No   Maybe

You only want to deal with the items which you have written YES next to. The NO or MAYBE items can wait for another day. Deal only with the YES items today.

Using one 3 x 5 card for each activity, write out the activity you will do. Such activities might include:

- Get a haircut
- Go to the bank
- Pray for ten minutes
- Spend 30 minutes cleaning the kitchen
- Write a thank-you note to Sally
- See Mary's soccer game
- Prepare dinner for tonight

After all your activities have been written on separate 3 x 5 cards, sort them by the order of priority (what needs to be done first, second, third, etc.). Concentrate on only one activity at a time. After each has been completed, you can either toss out the 3 x 5 card or place it on the bottom of the stack of cards. When your children or mate come home and want to know what you've done all day, you can read off the various activities and they will be impressed!

Every request that comes your way doesn't have to be answered YES. It's okay to say NO. *You* need to control your schedule and not let others plan it for you.

12 Ways to Put Off Procrastinating

> It is far better not to say you'll do
> something than to say you will and
> then not do it.
>
> —*Ecclesiastes 5:5*

*T*HE NATIONAL Procrastination Club was scheduled to meet in San Francisco in early 1991, but the meeting was canceled because they weren't able to plan it. Does that sound like you or a good friend or yours? Most of us are caught up in the no-action mode of not getting started.

Many of us self-talk ourselves into procrastinating. We say things like "I work best under pressure" or "The easy way is the best way" or "I can still go shopping and get the assignment completed on time." Does this sound familiar?

It's hard to measure procrastination because we measure performance by what we *do* and not by what we *don't do*. Procrastination becomes a problem when we neglect or delay doing those things that are important to us. Procrastination is the universal "effectiveness killer." Putting things off takes an enormous toll. Some of these include:

• *Continuous frustration.* We are always under the stress of frustration. We say things like "I hope," "I wish," "Maybe things

17

will get better," and other such negative self-talk. We're always going to get it together *tomorrow*.

• *Boredom*. Boredom is a way of life, and a great escape for not using present moments constructively. Choosing boredom as a way of life is merely another way that the procrastinator structures her time.

• *Impotent goals*. We never get around to accomplishing our goals. Our speech is loaded with "I'm gonna's." But we never get around to actually putting into action our gonna's.

• *Always having unsolved problems*. We feel like a fireman trying to put out new fires. As we have one almost out, another one starts. We don't actually put any fires all the way out, and we're always tired because nothing is resolved. Unsolved problems tend to create more problems.

• *Waste of the present*. The past is history and tomorrow is only a vision, but the procrastinator wastes *today*. She is always living for tomorrow, and when tomorrow comes she starts waiting again for tomorrow.

• *Unfulfilled life*. Procrastination is an immobilizer that blocks fulfillment. There is always tomorrow, so today never has to count for anything. We fill our daily voids with less desirable things just to fill the void.

• *Poor health*. We put off next month to have a checkup for that lump in our breast. Then it is too late. Or we drive too long on bald tires, until we have a costly accident because we have a blowout on the freeway.

• *A life of indecision*. When we put off decisions we are forfeiting important opportunities. By not being able to make decisions we allow ourselves to become slaves to our future rather than masters of it.

• *Poor human relationships*. The people in our family, at our church, and at our work become restless around us if we aren't capable of doing anything. People don't want to be around us. We become the object of jokes and insults, which damage our relationships over time.

• *Fatigue*. With all the above energy drains working against us, no wonder we're tired at the end of the day!

How to Roll into Action

A human body at rest tends to remain at rest, and a body in motion tends to remain in motion. Procrastinators have a difficult time getting in motion, but once we get into motion we tend to stay in motion. If we gain momentum the task is well on its way to completion.

The following are a few ideas for creating momentum.

1. *Recognize the futility of procrastination as a way of living.* Do you really want a life of frustration, fatigue, and boredom?

2. *Break down overwhelming tasks into small tasks.* Try to limit them to five-to-ten-minute tasks. Write them on 3 x 5 cards for easy referral. Hardly anything is really hard if you divide it into small jobs.

3. *Face unpleasant tasks squarely.* Ignoring unpleasant tasks doesn't make them go away. Not doing it today only insures that you will feel equally burdened about it (plus other tasks) tomorrow.

4. *Do a start-up task.* Pick one or two of those instant tasks from number 2 above and begin to work on those. Just get started.

5. *Take advantage of your moods.* If there are tasks you don't feel like doing today, find those tasks you *do* feel like doing today. Take advantage of your moods. Get started.

6. *Think of something important that you have been putting off.* List the good things that could possibly happen by doing the task. Now list the disadvantages that could come about as a result of inaction. You will usually find that the advantages outweigh the disadvantages.

7. *Make a commitment to someone.* Enlist a friend to hold you accountable for getting started. Choose someone who is firm and won't let you off the hook.

8. *Give yourself a reward.* Find an important goal that you have been dodging and decide what would be a fitting reward for you when you achieve it. Make your reward commensurate with the size of the task.

9. *Give yourself deadlines.* Color-code the due date on your calendar so you can visually see that date each day. You might even color-code a few immediate dates along the way to make sure you are on track. Write down the due date.

10. *Resolve to make every day count.* Treat each day as a treasure. Self-talk yourself into accomplishing something new each day. Live for *today* without always anticipating tomorrow.

11. *Be decisive and have the courage to act.* Many times we're crippled by "what if," "I'm gonna," "I wish," "I want," "I hope," and so on. Make something happen!

12. *Refuse to be bored.* Get out of the rut you're living in. Buy some flowers, cook a new dish, replace the familiar with the unfamiliar. Take time to smell a new rose.

13. *Practice doing absolutely nothing.* When you're avoiding getting started, go sit in a chair and do absolutely nothing until you are motivated to begin. Most of us are poor at the art of doing nothing. You'll soon find yourself eager to get moving.

14. *Ask yourself, "What's the best use of my time and energy right now?"* If that's not what you are doing, then switch to a higher priority. What you are doing might be good, but is it the best?

15. *Ask yourself, "What is the greatest problem facing me, and what am I going to do about it today?"* Plan your action and get into motion.

As Christian women, we are directed in Proverbs 31:15, "She gets up before dawn to prepare breakfast for her household, and plans the day's work for her servant girls." This means we are to be women of action. Treat each day as being precious. When it's gone, it never comes back to you.

How to Stop Saying "I'll Do It Tomorrow"

Commit your work to the Lord, and
then it will succeed.

—*Proverbs 16:3*

*A*RE THERE things you really want
and need to accomplish but keep putting off for another day? Do you often let little things slide until they pile up and become large problems? Guess what—there is hope. There are steps you can take to get going and get organized.

In reality most procrastinators suffer from nothing more than simple laziness. They just delay doing things that bore them.

The perfectionist puts off projects because if she cannot do it perfectly she won't do it at all. Susan is a typical example of a perfectionist. The things she does are exact, perfect, and "spit-shined." She analyzes her project, gathers her tools and materials, sets a time, and goes for it. However, Susan's house can be a total mess much of the time because she doesn't tackle part of a job. If she can't do it all and do it perfectly, she'd rather not do it at all. So because she doesn't have large blocks of time in her life, she gets very little accomplished.

We all at times put things off for later, but later may never come. Who loves to rake leaves every day? But if they don't get raked we may never see the front yard until spring. Reward yourself after those "hate-to-do" jobs. Take ten minutes to read a magazine or have a cup of tea or hot cocoa. Arrange some flowers or do something fun and something you love to do. Remember, life sometimes isn't easy; we have many responsibilities we may dislike doing.

Here are a few tips to help you get going.

1. *Set goals*. Set manageable goals. Start with small ones so that you feel a sense of accomplishment. If it's the hall closet that needs cleaning, plan to do it in three-to-fifteen-minute segments. If it's answering letters, don't do them all in one day; set a goal of 30 minutes a week until you're all caught up. Remember, break things up into small steps.

2. *Make a schedule*. Block out time for each day on your calendar to complete a task. Perhaps it's ironing; allot 30 minutes for the day, then STOP. Before long you will be all caught up. What you thought would take one whole day will only take 30 minutes a day for four days.

3. *Be realistic*. If you find that 30 minutes a day is too long, cut down the time by five or ten minutes. If you find that 30 minutes is not long enough, add ten or fifteen minutes. Remember that interruptions take place (children, phone, etc.), so be sure to allow for these.

4. *Take it easy*. If you feel overextended, trim down your commitments until you get caught up and have a workable, manageable load you can feel comfortable with.

5. *Get help*. Incorporate your family. Perhaps the garage or attic needs reorganizing. Ask, "What can you do to help mom and dad?" Plan a fun day working together, then reward the kids with their favorite chocolate cake and apple cider.

6. *Do it now*. Remember, it is more important to just *get it done now* than to do it perfectly later. *Now* gets results, and you'll feel great for accomplishing something.

7. *Be flexible with your goal*. Nothing is set in concrete. You may need to adjust your goals. Remember, setting a goal is a step in conquering procrastination.

8. *Remember to reward yourself along the way*. After that project is completed, all the letters answered, and the garage cleaned, get excited and take the family out to dinner or take a friend to lunch. How about an afternoon at the mall? Or feed the ducks with the children, ride bikes, fly kites, or cut pumpkins and make a pie. You know what you and your family love to do, so do it!

Give yourself time off. Even procrastinators deserve a little fun.

Thank the Lord each step of the way. God is interested in our successes and guides us through our failures.

Putting Everything in Its Place

There is an appointed time for
everything. And there is a time for
every event under heaven.

—*Ecclesiastes 3:1 NASB*

*W*ITH SPRING cleaning around the
corner, it's time to consider doing
something about the piles of stuff that have accumulated over the
winter days of holiday rush.

While we were busily celebrating Christmas and the New Year,
our closets, shelves, and drawers were mysteriously attracting all
sorts of odds and ends. These things have meaning to us and we don't
want to give or throw them away. But we do need places to put them
away. Here's a system that will get us organized.

The necessary basic equipment:

- 3 to 12 large cardboard boxes approximately 10 inches high, 12
  inches wide, and 16 inches long, lids preferred.
- One 3 x 5 plastic file card holder with 36 lined cards and seven
  divider tabs.
- One wide-tipped black felt marking pen.
- 8½ x 11 file folders

Take the large cardboard boxes and begin to fill them with the
items you want to save and store for future use.

Mark the front of each box with a number. Assign a 3 x 5 lined file card for each box. For each box write on the card what you have stored in that box. For example:

Box 1—Scrap sewing fabric
Box 2—Chad's baby toys and clothes
Box 3—Jenny's high school cheerleading uniform
Box 4—Ski clothes
Box 5—Gold-mining gear
Box 6—Snorkel gear with swim fins

Save Number 15 for your income tax records (April 15):

Box 15A—1987 records
Box 15B—1988 records
Box 15C—1989 records
Box 15D—1990 records
Box 15E—1991 records

Number 25 is a good one for your Christmas items:

Box 25A—Wreaths
Box 25B—Outdoor lights
Box 25C—Indoor lights
Box 25D—Tree decorations
Box 25E—Garlands & candles

By labeling your boxes A through Z you can add to your number sequence and keep all your items together. (It saves a lot of time when you need to retrieve those items.) Every two or three years go back through these boxes, cleaning them out and consolidating them.

On your 3 x 5 card write in the upper-right-hand corner where you have stored each box. Ideally, store these boxes in the garage, attic, or basement. If you don't have the luxury of lots of storage space, spray paint or wallpaper the boxes to fit in with the decor of your home (such as the laundry room, bedroom or bathroom).

When you get to the bottom of the "put away" pile, you will probably find many loose items of papers and records that need some type of storage for quick retrieval. This is where your 8½ x 11 file folders come in hand.

Label the folders with the following headings and then place each paper or receipt in the corresponding folder:

Insurance Papers
  • Auto
  • Health
  • Homeowner's
Homeowner Papers
  • Escrow papers
  • Tax records (for current year)

Receipts
- Auto repairs
- Major purchases

Store these folders in a metal file cabinet or a storage box. If possible, keep these boxes near the office area in your home. Close accessibility to these files will save you extra footsteps when you need to get to them.

Give your young children storage boxes, file cards, and file folders to help them keep their rooms organized. This provides an excellent model for their future personal organization.

Just think of your satisfaction when a member of your family comes to you and asks where something is and you pull out your box, flip through your cards, and tell him or her to look in Box 5, which is located under the attic stairs. Won't he be impressed with the new organized you!

Four Tools to an Organized You

To fail to plan is to plan to fail.
—*Unknown*

*D*O YOU EVER look around your home, room, or office and just want to throw up your hands in disgust and say, "It's no use, I'll never get organized"? The old saying "Everything has a place and everything in its place" sounds great, but how do you make it work for you? Here are four simple tools to help you get your home organized for the new year.

- "To do" list
- Calendar
- Telephone/address list
- Simple filing system

A "To Do" List

Use the same size of paper for the first three tools ($8\frac{1}{2}$ x 11 or $5\frac{1}{2}$ x $8\frac{1}{2}$). This way you won't have to fight with different sizes of paper. After choosing your size of paper, write the words TO DO at the top of a piece of paper. Begin writing down all the things that you need to do.

When you finish each item during the day, relish the pleasure of crossing it off the list. At the end of the day, review your list and update any new things you need to add. If you have accomplished something that day that wasn't on your list, write it down. Everyone's life is full of interruptions, and you need to applaud yourself for what you *did* accomplish!

At the end of the week, consolidate your lists and start again on Monday with a fresh page. Eventually you will want to rank your TO DO items by importance. This added technique will help you maximize your time to it fullest potential.

A Calendar

I recommend two types of calendars. The first is a two-page "Month at a Glance" calendar. One glance will give you a good idea of the overview of the month. Details aren't written here, but do jot down broad engagements with times. For example, write down meetings, luncheons, basketball games, speaking engagements, and dental appointments.

The second type of calendar is a page for each day—"A Day at a Glance." On this calendar you write down more specific details, such as what you will be doing on the hour or half-hour. Be careful that you don't overload your calendar and jam your appointments too close together. Remember to schedule in time alone and time with God.

As a guideline, I suggest that if you've been someplace before and you know where you're going, allow 25 percent more time than you think it will take. If you estimate that a meeting will last one hour, block out one hour and fifteen minutes.

A Telephone/Address List

This list will become your personal telephone and address book. Using the same size paper as your TO DO list and calendar, design your own directory of information for home, work, and play. You might want to list certain numbers by broad headings, such as schools, attorneys, dentists, doctors, plumbers, carpenters, and restaurants. This helps you look up the specifics when you can't remember the person's last name. Use a pencil in writing down addresses and telephone numbers; since it is much easier to correct than ink if the information changes.

If you have a client or customer listed, you may want to mark down personal data about the person to review before your next meeting.

Some items to include are the client's spouse and children's names, sports of interest, and favorite foods and vacation spots. Your clients will be impressed that you remembered all that information about them.

The same system works well with guests in your home. Include some of the meals you served them, any particular food allergies they have, and whether they drank coffee or tea.

A Simple Filing System

The motto in our home is "Don't pile it, file it." This tool will make your home look like a new place! At your local stationery store, purchase about four dozen colored or manila 8½ x 14 file folders. I recommend colored file folders because they help you categorize your material and also add a little cheer to your day. I find that the legal-size folder (8½ x 14) are more functional, since they accommodate longer, nonstandardized pieces of paper.

Label each folder with a simple heading, such as Sales Slips, Auto, Insurance, School Papers, Maps, Warranties, Taxes, and Checks. Then take all the loose papers you find around your home and put them into their respective folders. If you have a filing cabinet to house these folders, that's great. If not, just get a cardboard storage box to get started.

After you have mastered these four tools to organization, you can branch out and acquire more skills. Remember, though, to give yourself time, since it takes 21 consecutive days to acquire a new habit.

How to Find More Time

All of us must quickly carry out the
tasks assigned to us by [God] . . .
for there is little time left before
the night falls.

—*John 9:4*

*I*F ONLY I could get organized!" "I
just don't have enough time in the day!"
Do you ever hear yourself making these statements?

Don't we all at some point in our lives find ourselves waiting until the last minute to fill out tax forms, wrap Christmas presents, or send a belated birthday card?

Here are a few ideas that will help you find more time for yourself and enable you to get all those little jobs done.

1. As you make a TO DO list, set small, manageable deadlines for yourself. For example, by October 2 I'll clean two drawers in the kitchen. By October 8 I'll sort through papers in my desk. On October 28 I'll select my Christmas cards.

Some other bite-sized chunks that will take 15 minutes a day are answering a letter, cleaning a bathroom, or changing the linen on one bed. If it helps, set a timer for 15 minutes. When the timer goes off, go back to your regular schedule.

2. Plan ahead for guests. Sometimes having guests come to your home can be overwhelming when you think about the preparation

involved. Doing things in 15-minute increments works wonders for your preparation. Write out a TO DO list about a week before your party, Sunday brunch, or arrival of weekend guests. Plan to do a little each day until your guests arrive.

For example, one day make up their bed with clean sheets. Wait until the next day to do the vacuuming and the following to do the baking. Remember, reward yourself or give yourself a break after each accomplishment. Pick some flowers, take a walk, polish your nails, or give yourself a facial.

3. Watch out for interruptions. They will be there, but try to avoid them. If you have an answering machine, turn it on. If you don't have a machine, tell the caller you will call back later, when you finish the project you're involved in. Wait until the baby is sleeping for certain projects. Put a note on the front door that reads "Available after 3 P.M."

4. Learn to say no at least until you've completed what you set out to do on your list. But remember to keep your list realistic and obtainable. Don't load yourself to the point that you feel overwhelmed and then give up and do nothing at all.

5. Get your family to help with odd jobs by giving them a chart. TO DO BY 5 P.M.: a) Sweep the driveway; b) Rake the leaves in the backyard; c) Set the table for the next meal; d) Take an apple break.

Let your family in on your 15-minute plan. They'll love working against time; it becomes a game. Reward, praise, and compliment them for a job well done. If each child works 15 minutes a day toward an organized home, look how many hours it will save you! This will give you time for yourself and at the same time teach your children to be responsible young people.

6. Reward yourself when projects are complete. Go out for lunch with a friend and share what you've accomplished. She'll be excited for you and probably go home and clean out her drawers too! Or sit down with a cup of tea or coffee and read a magazine or the Bible.

Cleaning

8

How to Get Housework Done in Record Time

> Teach us to number our days and recognize how few they are; help us to spend them as we should.
> —*Psalm 90:12*

*F*OR THE BUSY woman today, housework is a nuisance and not necessarily her real concern. Today's woman does not have time to devote her full time to cleaning, as did her grandmother. However, dirt doesn't just blow away and seven dwarfs don't appear at night while we sleep to clean up our messes. Wouldn't it be wonderful to have time to do things with family and church instead of spending all day Saturday cleaning, cleaning, cleaning? Here are some speedy tips to get the job done and feel great about doing it.

Start with collecting the right supplies.

• Pail or bucket and mop.

• Broom and dustpan.

• Squeegee. Professionals use these exclusively. Never use newspaper or paper towels, since they contain fibers that leave the windows messy. A good squeegee works fast and easy: Use a spray bottle with rubbing alcohol; spray on window and squeegee off.

• Billy's old football knee pads. These are great protectors which can be purchased at sporting goods stores (or similar work pads at hardware stores) for cleaning floors and tubs. Soft pads keep knee work less painful.

• Clean dustcloths. Diapers are great, and so are 100 percent cotton dishcloths (well-washed and dried).

• Carry-all tray. A must for storing cleaning items such as wax, window spray, etc.

• Feather duster. A super item for moving small amounts of dust from a higher level to a lower level, where most of it can be vacuumed up. I have lots of cobwebs and knickknack items, and this is my quick lifesaver of dusting each item every time. Invest in a good ostrich duster. You can purchase one at a hardware or janitor supply store.

• Pumice stone. It gets that ugly ring out of the toilet bowl caused by rust and mineral deposits. It's amazing how fast a pumice stone will remove the scale; just rub it on the ring gently and it's gone. It also cleans ovens and removes the carbon buildup on grills and iron cookware, as well as removing paint from concrete and masonry walls and scale from swimming pools. Pumice stones can be purchased in hardware stores, janitor supply stores, and beauty supply stores.

• Toothbrush. Great for cleaning the hard corners of floors and showers and around faucets at the sink.

• Vacuum cleaner. An absolute must!

• Ammonia. An excellent cleaner (not the sudsy type) for floors.

• Powdered cleanser. For sinks and bathtubs.

• Oven cleaner.

• Rubber gloves. To protect your hands from the chemicals in household cleaners and detergents.

• Scraper. Use the razor-blade type to remove paint from tile or glass and decals or stickers from the shower door. Also, remove dried-on food after it gets hard, such as pancake batter or eggs. But be careful not to scratch the surface.

Fill your carry-all tray with many of the above items. It's ready to work when you are!

When you work, be sure to use the SPEEDY EASY METHOD:

1. Put on some music with a very fast beat. This will help your cleaning go faster plus take your mind off the drudgery.

2. Go in one direction. Work around your room from top to bottom and from right to left or left to right—whatever feels good to you. Also start at one end of your home and work toward the other end. Don't get sidetracked with this mess and that mess.

3. Before cleaning windowpanes, wipe or vacuum sills and wood cross-frames. Use your spray bottle with alcohol and squeegee and

cotton cloth. Use a horizontal stroke on the outside and a vertical stroke on the inside. That way you'll know if you missed a spot because you can tell which side the streak is on.

4. Use your hair dryer to blow off the dust from silk flowers. Your feather duster will work well to dust off soft fabric items, plants, picture frames, and lampshades. Remember, we're working from top to bottom in each room, so you'll be vacuuming up this dust soon.

5. After wiping clean your wastebaskets, give the inside bottom a quick coat of floor wax. This will prevent trash from sticking to the bottom of the wastebasket in the future.

6. Change your air conditioner and heater filters every six months for best performance. This will keep the dust and dirt from circulating through your rooms.

7. Wipe off the blades of your window and/or room fans quarterly to keep dirt and dust from flying around.

8. Try to avoid interruptions; take the phone message and call back when it is convenient.

9. Big question: Should you vacuum first or last? Last, of course.

Having the proper tools helps. Don't feel that everything has to be done in one work session. Set your timer and then work in 15-minute time slots. Work fast, but after each time and/or project, treat yourself to a cup of hot chocolate or iced tea, or put a mask on your face and enjoy a hot bath.

Then go to the garden and pick a fresh bouquet of flowers for your beautiful clean house.

Are You
a Pack Rat?

She watches carefully all that goes
on throughout her household, and is
never lazy.

—Proverbs 31:27

*A*NSWER YES OR NO to each question. You get a zero for every no and one point for every yes.

A zero is a perfect score and probably impossible. If your score is 10, you are a pack rat and you've come to the right place!

1. Do you find yourself complaining that you don't have enough room or space?

2. Do you have things piled up in cupboards and closets or stacked into corners because there is no place to put them?

3. Do you have magazines stacked around the house waiting to be read? Are you saving them for the day when you'll sit down and cut out articles, recipes, and patterns?

4. Do things often get "lost" in your house?

5. Do you think, "I'll just put this here for now and put it away later"?

6. Are things collecting on top of your refrigerator, dresser drawers in the bedroom, counters, end tables, coffee tables, and bookshelves?

7. Do you have things around your home that you haven't used for a long time or possibly don't even want?

8. Do you ever buy something you already have at home because you can't find it or don't want to look for it?

9. Do you often say, "It might come in handy someday"?

10. Do you have to move things around in your closet or cupboards to find a certain item?

Let's see how you did.

0-3	You're in pretty good shape.
4-7	You could use some improvement.
8-10	It's never too late, pack rat. However, I'd start with prayer. Philippians 4:13 says, "I can do all things through Christ who strengthens me" (NKJV).

Begin with a family meeting, saying that you have discovered a problem. Let them know that you are a collector of things and need help from all of them, along with their support, to help you get your house in order.

When we admit our problem, somehow it helps us to get started in organizing.

You didn't get to this problem point by yourself; surely the whole family is as guilty as you are. But *you* are the one admitting it, so let's start with you. You take the responsibility and work toward getting control. (Altogether too many homes today are controlling us instead of us being in control of our homes.)

Step 1 is to think of what area of your clutter is bothering you the most. Is it the top of the refrigerator?

Step 2 is to set a 10-to-15-minute time slot to take care of that clutter. Set your timer on the oven and go at it. You'll be surprised at what you can get done in 15-minute intervals!

Repeat steps 1 and 2 above with each area of your home clutter. It may take weeks to finish the project, but at least you'll be working toward organizing your pack rat clutter.

Begin to file away the piles of papers, letters, articles, etc. into a file cabinet or cardboard file box, keeping in mind **DON'T PUT IT DOWN, PUT IT AWAY!**

This will help you in the future to put things in their proper place.

If you have a difficult time deciding whether to *throw* something away or *store* it away, put those difficult-decision things into a box or baggie and put it in the garage, attic, or basement. Then if something is so important to you that you would go to the extreme of retrieving it from the box or baggie, that item should be stored nearby. But if those boxes or bags sit for several months untouched, it's a sure indication to give them away or throw them away.

"Out of sight, out of mind" is a good saying to remember. So *throw away* and *give away*.

After attending one of my seminars, one woman told me that in five weeks she had organized the things in her home into 62 cardboard boxes! She said, "I'm a pack rat, but at least I'm an organized one!"

Key to a Clean House

In everything you do, put God first,
and he will direct you and crown
your efforts with success.
—*Proverbs 3:6*

*D*O YOU HAVE the type of home where every room you go into contains so many odd jobs to do (picking up yesterday's paper, washing off the refrigerator door, folding the last load of clothes) that you rush around all day never completing any one job?

If you struggle with getting household chores done, try this time-tested technique: *Break down big jobs into little jobs*. Here are a few ideas.

• Commit yourself to accomplishing a chore that shows. Start by picking up and putting away items in the living room that don't belong there (i.e., last week's TV listings or your son's Tonka truck). It will help you feel better if, as you walk into the house, at least the living room is in order. Take a minute to make a bed or pick up dirty dishes scattered throughout the house. The idea is to organize *at least one thing*, since this will take you only two minutes or less.

• *Buy a timer or use the one on your oven.* A woman once told me that she hated to mop her kitchen floor. It caused her anger and stress every time she thought of doing it, and even more stress every time she walked across a sticky floor.

I recommended that she time how long it took her to mop her floor. She reported that it only took her three minutes! Now when she thinks of mopping that floor she thinks of taking only three minutes to do the job, and she feels less stressed about it. We have many jobs around our homes that can be done in three to ten minutes.

• *List on a piece of paper the jobs that can be done in 15 minutes or less.* This will be easy to do once you get into the swing of timing your chores.

Because our normal tendency is to group work into big jobs, we make the excuse that we don't have time to do certain chores. For example, we may figure it takes 30 minutes to clean the refrigerator, and if we don't have 30 minutes to do it, we won't do it at all.

In reality it could take only seven minutes. Once you've timed this job, the next time the refrigerator needs cleaning it won't be that big a deal.

• *Profit from the precious minutes usually wasted while you wait for someone.* You are ready for Marci to pick you up for that meeting, but you have ten minutes before she comes. Instead of sitting on the stairs to wait for her, look around and find one simple task you can complete. One glance and you'll find jobs such as unloading the dishwasher, dusting a table, folding a load of laundry, putting a fresh load of clothes in the washer, or wiping around the bathroom sink.

• *Divide jobs into segments.* When cleaning the living room, divide it into three segments: dusting, picking up items, and vacuuming. The segment idea also goes for the bathroom: scrubbing the sink, shower, and toilet; mopping the floor; shaking out the throw rugs; polishing the mirrors.

• *Improve a room's appearance every time you go into it.* Simply putting the milk away or straightening a bath towel will make the room look better, and then you'll feel better about it. Remember, don't put it *down*, put it *away*.

• *Replace an item where it belongs after you use it.* (This is one idea that would be worth training the whole family to do.) Instead of leaving the toothpaste cap on the counter, put it back on the tube and place the toothpaste in a drawer or on the shelf.

Instead of tossing a towel on the floor or clothing on the bed, hang it back up on the towel rack, or on a hanger in the closet.

• *Do simple tasks right away.* For example, if you go to the grocery store and buy celery, don't put off cleaning it. Instead, as you're putting away your groceries, clean the celery, cut it up, put it in a container of water, and slip it into the refrigerator. Presto, the job is done!

This week commit yourself to nine things you can do in 15-minute time slots. When you do, you'll have accomplished 1½ hours of cleaning without even noticing it!

Do I Really Need This?

Teach a wise man, and he will be
wiser; teach a good man and he
will learn more.

—*Proverbs 9:9*

I HAVE A FRIEND who has 40 robes.
Now one woman cannot possibly wear
40 robes. "It's hard to throw things out," she says. Another woman
has saved her plastic baggies from the supermarket and at last count
had 320 of them!

We live in a world of mass production and marketing. We must
learn to sort and let go of certain things, or else we will need to build
a huge warehouse to contain everything, not to mention inventorying
the stock of collectibles so we know what we have and where it all is
located. Years ago, when we got something we kept it until it wore
out. But today it may never wear out before we tire of it. Yet it seems
just too good to dispose of.

We often have things not because of an active decision to keep
them but because we have not made the decision to get rid of them.

On an average, people keep things several years after their usefulness has passed. Perhaps we overbuy and have supplies, materials, and
tools left over. The things we liked years ago are not what we like or
enjoy today, but we hang onto them, thinking that someday we may use

them again. It's like we're obligated to keep them "just in case."

Toys and baby equipment are saved because someday they may be used for grandchildren. We store things for our adult children "someday."

Let's face the job of streamlining our possessions and ask ourselves some questions:

1. How long has it been since you used that item? My rule of thumb is if it hasn't been used in the past year I'm going to give it away, throw it away, or store it away.

I use trash bags for my throwaway items. A black one is best so *you* can't see in it, *your husband* can't see in it, and *your children* can't see in it. Those 320 baggies can go into the throwaway bags, along with broken toys, torn and stained clothing, and newspapers and jars you've been saving for the "someday" you might use them.

Keep tax records (including canceled checks) for seven years and then throw them out. (But keep *homebuying* and *homeselling* records permanently.) Throw out most receipts, check stubs, and utility bills after two or three years.

2. The irreplaceable items that I don't use go into storage boxes, such as my honeymoon suit, Bob's high school or college letterman's jackets, baby's first shoes, and other memorabilia. Those boxes I number 1, 2, 3, etc. I catalog these on a 3 x 5 card that is also numbered, and I put it into a small file box. Then these cards are ready to retrieve if I need them at a later date.

3. The only reasons to keep things for long periods should be for memories or perhaps to pass on to another member in the family someday, such as a lace tablecloth, a quilt, granddad's toolbox or pocket knife, or books that can benefit another member of the family or a friend.

Things you don't need to keep include old magazines (unless they could realistically become collector's items) or magazines that are recent. These could be placed in your doctor's office, convalescent hospitals, etc. Junk mail is a big source of clutter and needs to be thrown away. *"Don't put it away, throw it away"* is a good motto for that junk mail. If you have a pile now, stop and throw it away right now. It's a great feeling, isn't it? But a new pile will return in a few days, so do it again and again until you realize that throwing this junk mail away is not going to affect your life in any way other than making you feel great!

With other mail our motto is *"File it, don't pile it!"* Get some file folders and label them "Medical," "Insurance," "Bills," "Household," "Letters to Answer," etc. As the mail comes in, open it, read it, quickly highlight it with a yellow pen, and then file it into the proper folders. Those folders can then go into a file drawer or box.

Our children's school papers were kept for one week, with two papers chosen at the end of the week and put into a file folder. At the end of the month they were allowed to choose only two special "let's keep" papers. By the end of the year the file folder consisted of those special papers, photos, and report cards. Each year the folder was put into their own "keepsake" box, and by the time high school graduation came each person had a special box filled with special memories. (They still have these boxes.)

On my fiftieth birthday I received over 150 cards, each one from a special friend, with special notes in many cases. They would fill a box just by themselves. Not too many people are interested in those cards except me, and in 20 years certainly no one but me. With those that I could, I cut off the front side of the card and used them as postcards (if not written on). Special notes I kept and put into a memorable photo book with my birthday celebration pictures.

Cards that Bob and the children have sent me over the years I keep in a file folder, being careful only to keep those that are unusual or have notes. Now . . . hold your breath . . . I dumped all the others!

If you or your husband or your children are pack rats, use my box and catalog system for storage. You may still be a pack rat, but at least you'll be an organized one!

Swish, Swash,
How Do I Wash?

She is energetic, a hard worker.
—*Proverbs 31:17*

I WAS TALKING with a woman who had 15 children (all single births) who told me she pulled 60 socks out of her dryer one day and none of them matched! I was able to tell her about those plastic sock sorters you can buy that scoot onto the end of a pair of socks. Into the washer and dryer then go, and they stay together until you are ready to roll them and put them in a drawer. I have also had women tell me they keep a good supply of large safety pins by their laundry area so they can safety pin the socks together in pairs before putting them into the washer.

It has always amazed me how socks get totally lost from the washer to the dryer, and come out single and perhaps lost forever. I'm beginning to think that our appliances feed on socks, since they seem to get eaten in the laundry process!

The laundry needs organization as much as any other area of our homes.

In raising our children, I delegated much of the chores to the children themselves. By the time Jenny was ten years old she was doing all the laundry from sorting to ironing. It took time and training to get her to that point, however. I didn't just dump the laundry responsibility in her lap at ten years old and tell her to go to it. I began when they were two and three teaching both Jenny and Brad to sort the dirty clothes into three laundry bags. One was a colored bag made out of some bright calico print fabric that had lots of colors on it; all the *colored* clothes went into that bag. Another laundry bag was all white for the *white* clothes, and another one was navy or dark solid for the dirty *dark-colored* clothes.

Make a rule that what goes in the wash inside out (such as socks, underwear, and T-shirts) comes out inside out. Have everyone straighten his or her own clothes. King-size pillowcases make great laundry bags. You can string some shoe laces around the top and you have laundry bags—fast, simple, and not too expensive, if you buy the pillowcases on sale. Colored plastic trash cans make great laundry sorters also. With a fat felt pen you can write on the outside "COLORED," "WHITE," or "DARK." That way the family can simply sort their dirty clothes as they dump them in the proper bins.

Now that the clothes have been sorted and the socks paired up with your sock sorters, you can plan your washday.

Young mothers with several children may need to wash every day, others one to three times per week. But it is important to schedule your laundry days ahead and begin early in the day, or better yet, put in a load the night before. Many days I would have a load started the night before. On your way to bed, simply dump in one of the bags of sorted clothes. By morning they are ready to put into the dryer or basket for hanging out today, and you will be one load ahead of the game. When it was Jenny's responsibility for the laundry, I would put a load in on my way to bed as a little surprise to help her out with the chores.

If at all possible, use cold water, especially on colored clothes. The colors stay sharp longer and don't fade as quickly.

Wash full loads rather than small loads. That saves on energy for both you and the appliances. Remember, *do not* run the washing machine or dryer when no one is at home. If the machine leaks or shirt-circuits, you could have some big problems.

As soon as the dryer stops, take out the permanent press articles. Think toward no ironing, and that way you'll have less ironing than otherwise. Many articles can go without the iron if you remove them immediately from the dryer and put them on hangers. So . . . keep a good supply of hangers close to your laundry area!

Now let's talk about hangers. The plastic colored-type are really the best. They help prevent marks and creases on your clothing, plus you can color-code your whole family. If you have several children at home, plus mom and dad, you will use a lot of hangers.

An easy way it worked for us was to give each person in the family a color. Brad had blue, Jenny had yellow, mom had white, dad had red, etc. When the shirts or blouses were taken out of the dryer, they were hung on the appropriate-colored hangers. Then when the children came in from school, they picked up the hangers of their color, took them to their room, and hung them up.

You can also color-code underwear and socks as much as possible by giving each family member his or her color or pattern. Another great idea is to sew onto the garments (with a thread or embroidery thread) the person's color so he or she can identify the items. Color-coding also works well with folded clothes. One mom told me she had a shelf built in her laundry area, and on this shelf she placed colored plastic bins (the dishpan type). So if Brad's color is blue he gets a blue bin, Jenny gets yellow, etc. All the folded-type clothes go in at the time of folding and are taken to the person's room. If the bin is not returned to the laundry area, then no clean clothes until it is!

Another mom went a step further and gave each person his own colored towels. Again, Brad would now have blue towels. If a towel is left lying around and it's blue, we know who didn't hang up his towel or put it away!

Put a few hooks near the laundry area so they will be handy to hang the colored hangers on. If your laundry area is in the garage, a long nail works great. Or string a line from one rafter to the next. (It also makes a great clothesline for those drip-dry articles or rainy day hangups.)

Fold each load as you take it out of the dryer. Should you forget a load and it sets awhile, simply throw in a well-dampened towel and let it dry again for about ten minutes. The dampness from the towel will freshen up the load and take out any set wrinkles.

Set aside at least one day a week for ironing. Keeping ahead of ironing is the only way to keep your mind free of those "need to do" lists that grow longer and longer.

One husband shared with me that anytime he needed a fresh shirt to wear, it needed to be ironed. Surprise him, gals, and have a catch-up ironing day! How happy he will be when he goes to the closet and see *all* his shirts beautifully ironed on his colored hangers! Then keep it up. No more hurried ironing at 6:00 A.M. so hubby has a clean shirt to wear to work. It's another way of saying "I love you."

When folding linens and towels, fold them all in one direction. When they are placed on the linen closet shelf, they can be piled up neatly in an organized fashion.

Label your shelves in the linen closet so that whoever puts the linens away will know the right spot.

Buying different patterned sheets for each person's bed is great for instant recognition. One mother told me she buys solid sheets for twin beds, stripes for full or queen, and floral for the king-sized beds.

Let's Review

- Teach and delegate some laundry responsibilities to your family.
- Start washing loads early in the day or the night before.
- Color-code the family.
- Aim toward having no ironing.
- Fold each load as you take it out of the dryer.
- Iron weekly to prevent ironing build-up.
- Have family members put away their own laundry.
- Label linen-closet shelves for quick identification.
- Thank the Lord we have appliances to help us save time!

Household Remedies for Stubborn Stains

A home is built of loving deeds.

 *H*OLIDAY TIME is busy enough without having to fight spots and stains. Do you wonder how you can get stubborn stains out? If the holiday tablecloth is stained and so are the cloth napkins—with lipstick—this can cause added stress for the holidays as well as any day.

Here are some hints on getting those stubborn stains out.

Candle wax. To remove from fabrics, simply place a paper towel under the spot and one on top of the spot. Press with a warm iron until the paper towel absorbs the melted wax. Move the paper towel frequently so it doesn't oversaturate.

Coffee or tea. Can be removed by rubbing the stain with a damp cloth dipped in baking soda.

Lipstick. Here are three ways to remove lipstick from fabric: 1) Rub it with a slice of white bread; 2) dab the smear with petroleum jelly, then apply a dry-cleaning solution; 3) pat with salad oil on the spot and launder the fabric after five minutes.

Makeup marks disappear from dark clothing if they are rubbed with bread.

Nail polish spots. If they get on fabric (which happens often to women with small children), lift the spot by applying remover to the fabric underside. (But first check on an inconspicuous place to make sure you won't damage the fabric.)

Grease. Remove grease from fabrics by applying cornstarch or dampening and then adding salt dissolved in ammonia.

Food stains. There are several ways to remove chocolate or cocoa stains from fabrics. You could soak the stains thoroughly with club soda before washing or else rub talcum powder into the stains to absorb them. Try applying milk to the stains, since milk keeps them from setting. A fourth way is to rub shortening into them, then launder. Remove fruit stains by pouring a mixture of detergent and boiling water through the fabric or sponge the stained area with lemon juice. You can also rub the cut sides of a lemon slice over the stain. To remove egg stains from fabric, soak the fabric for an hour in cold water before laundering.

Hardened stains. These can sometimes be loosened up by placing a pad dampened with stain remover on top of the stain and keeping the top pad damp by adding more stain remover as needed.

You can remove shoe polish from clothing by applying rubbing alcohol. If traces of polish remain, add a teaspoon of borax powder to the water when laundering.

To eliminate a tar spot on fabric, apply shortening and let the tar soften for ten mintues. Scrape it away and launder.

Hints on Treating Spots and Stains

Work fast! Treat the stains right away. The longer a stain stays on a fabric, the more likely it is to become permanent.

Handle stained items gently. Rubbing, folding, wringing, or squeezing can cause the stain to penetrate more deeply and may damage delicate fibers.

Keep a cool approach to stain removal, since heat can set a stain. Keep stained fabrics away from hot water, a dryer, or an iron. After washing a garment, be sure all stains are completely removed *before* ironing. Heat-set stains are often impossible to remove.

Remove as much of a stain-producing agent as possible before treating it with a stain-removal product. That way you'll avoid the the possibility of enlarging the stain.

Steps to Success

Pretest any stain-removing agent in an inconspicuous spot, such as the seam allowance or hem of a garment, the part of a rug that is hidden under a table or chair, or the upholstery under a seat cushion. Always run a sample test, since even water may damage some surfaces.

When you flush a stain, especially on a nonwashable fabric, carefully control the flow of flushing liquid with an adjustable plastic trigger spray bottle.

When stain-remover instructions call for sponging, place the fabric stained-side-down on an absorbent pad. Then dampen another pad with water or a stain remover and blot lightly from the center of the stain outward to the edge to minimize the formation of rings. Change the absorbent pads when there is any sign of the stain transferring to them so the stain won't be redeposited on the fabric. For ring-prone fabrics, barely touch the stain with the sponging pad so the stain absorbs the cleaner slowly. When the spot has been lifted, use a dry pad on either side to blot up as much excess moisture as possible.

Tamping is a good way to remove stains if the fabric is sturdy enough. Use a small dry brush or toothbrush. Use it as a small hammer with a light action until the stain is removed.

An effective way to loosen many stains is by scraping with a teaspoon. Place the stain directly on the work surface and grasp the spoon by the side of its bowl. After adding a stain remover to the stain, move the edge of the spoon's bowl back and forth in short strokes, without pressing hard on the spoon. This procedure shouldn't be used on delicate fabrics.

You'll get best results if you work from the center of the stain outward.

If, in the cleaning process, you have to use more than one stain-removal agent or method, thoroughly rinse after each one before applying the next.

Homemade Spot Removers

A soapless spot cleaner can be created by mixing two cups of isopropyl rubbing alcohol (70%) with ¾ cup of white vinegar. Pour the mixture into a clean bottle and cover tightly. *Label* the bottle. To use, blot the soiled area until it is dry, apply the cleaner with a cloth or sponge and let stand for several minutes, then blot the area dry again. Repeat if necessary. Blot with water after using.

To make a wet spotter for nongreasy stains, combine one cup of water with two tablespoons of glycerin and two tablespoons of liquid dishwashing detergent. Stir in a small bowl until the mixture is thoroughly blended. Pour into a clean bottle or squeeze bottle and cover the container tightly. *Label*. When using, blot the soiled area dry, apply the spotter, let the spotter stand for several minutes, and then blot the soiled area dry again. Repeat if necessary.

Tips
for Easier
Spring Cleaning

In everything you do, put God first,
and he will direct you and crown
your efforts with success.

—*Proverbs 3:6*

$\mathcal{A}$S WINTER begins to melt away, we get excited and motivated to get our homes in order. But it takes a bit of organization and a few tips in order to get started toward completing the job. Just remember, it can take less time than you think. Jobs that you anticipate taking two hours can actually take only a few minutes.

So let's get started with these three thoughts in mind:

> DO IT!
> > DO IT RIGHT!
> > > DO IT RIGHT NOW!

Cleaning Products to Have on Hand

- All-purpose cleaner
- Floor products (waxes plus cleaners for vinyl or wood floors)
- Bathroom products (disinfectant, tile cleaner, mildew remover)
- Furniture polish
- Cleaning pads

- Scouring powders
- Metal polish
- Silver polish
- Window cleaner
- Dishwashing detergent or powder
- Rug and carpet cleaners
- Upholstery cleaners (Scotchguard after cleaning to protect against staining)
- Bleach, liquid or dry
- Fabric softener, liquid or sheets
- Prewash stain removers
- Oven cleaner (be sure to use rubber gloves with this type of cleaner)
- Drain cleaner
- Toilet bowl cleaner (a pumice stone is a must for removing the ring around the bowl)
- General cleaners (vinegar, ammonia, baking soda)

Cleaning Tools to Have on Hand

- Rubber gloves
- Vacuum cleaner, plus attachments for those hard-to-reach places (blinds, baseboards, radiators, shutters, corners in furniture, mattresses, ceilings, and walls)
- Dustcloth (100% cotton is best, such as towels, flannel, etc.)
- Feather duster
- Brushes for corners, tile, barbecue, etc.
- Paper towels
- Bucket
- Rags
- Broom and dustpan
- Stepladder or stepstool
- Mop
- Floor polisher or shampoo rug cleaner (optional)

Methods to Try

- Do one room at a time. Don't hurry; be thorough.
- Make a chart and delegate some of the jobs to the family: a) dad: windows; b) son: barbecue; c) daughter: pantry.
- Each week reward your family by making their favorite pie, cake, or dinner.
- Take short breaks and eat an apple or have a cup of tea or chocolate milk and cookies.

- Take cleaners with you from job to job and room to room by putting them in a bucket, a plastic type carry-all, or a basket.
- Turn on the radio for music to work by. Make it lively music so you can work faster.
- Time yourself by setting a timer. It's amazing what you can accomplish in 15 minutes.
- Upholstery furniture pieces can be brushed and vacuumed clean. This removes surface dirt and should be done four times a year.
- Drapes can be sent out for cleaning, or, depending on their fabric, they could be washed. Once-a-year cleaning is generally enough.
- Miniblinds can be removed and hosed down with sudsy water and ammonia. Then they can be maintained monthly with a feather duster.
- Wash windows quarterly (more often if needed).
- Baseboards should be checked monthly and cleaned if needed.
- Check air conditioner/heating unit. The filters need to be checked and replaced at least twice a year. These must be kept clean for maximum efficiency and lowest cost.
- Barbecue grill can be scrubbed with a hard brush. Oven cleaner works great, but make sure to use rubber gloves. Remember to remove ashes after each use.
- Keep your awnings clean by scrubbing with a long-handle brush. Use water and a mild soap. Rinse with a hose.
- Garage and cement driveways can be cleaned and scrubbed with detergent. Scrub with a stiff broom dipped in thick detergent suds. Repeat over the oil stains. Rinse by hosing with clean water.

Organizing Your Summer to Prevent Trouble

> They that wait upon the Lord shall renew their strength. They shall mount up with wings like eagles.
> —*Isaiah 40:31*

*T*HE NATIONAL Safety Council estimates that more than half of all summer accidents could be prevented if people took simple, common-sense precautions.

Summer brings varied schedules and activities: day and summer camp, skiing, swimming, biking, and many other activities which may result in animal bites, heat exposure, sunburn, cuts, insect bites, and much more. Unpredictable situations may be prevented by following these helpful hints:

• Post emergency phone numbers in plain view by the telephone for you and your children and the babysitter.

• Plan ahead by taking a first-aid class including CPR (cardiopulmonary resuscitation) from your local Red Cross chapter. Many chapters offer the classes at no charge.

• Give your children swimming lessons at the earliest possible age. Many YMCA's and YWCA's offer great programs for children.

• If you are in an area where no swimming classes are offered, work with your children yourself. We started with our children at a very young age by pouring water over their heads and having them hold their breath and blow bubbles underwater. Make it fun, and at the same time you will be helping them become comfortable in water.

• Common water-safety violations often result in injury. These include running, jumping, or sliding around a pool deck, diving without checking the water depth, and leaving a child unattended beside a pool, lake, or bathtub. (Purchase a cordless phone to keep with you at home so you won't leave the children unattended by pool or bathtub.) Go over safety rules with the family *often*: no running, never swim alone, etc.

• Purchase (or put together yourself) a first-aid kit for car travel. Keep it in a suitcase at the lake or pool area. This will keep it handy for you but out of the reach of children.

• Sunburn is very common, so use extra precautions. Sunscreen lotions are a must; keep them handy for small children and light-skinned people. Sunscreens are rated from 1 to 30; the higher the number, the more protection they give. A sun hat, visor, or bonnet is also recommended to prevent sunburned noses.

• Poison ivy, poison oak, and poison sumac are often found in uncultivated fields and wooded areas. Touching one of these plants (whose leaves often cluster three to a stalk) usually results within 24 hours in an oozy, itchy rash that may spread over much of the body. The trouble comes with infection caused by scratching the area. If your summer plans include hiking or picnicking in wooded or mountain areas, review with the family the facts about these poisonous plants. You may want to go to the library and find photos of the plants. Ask questions and inquire about these and other potential dangers in the area you plan to go to. Educate yourself and your family for a safer outing.

• Insect bites or stings can cause swelling, pain, redness, burning, or itching which can last from 48 to 72 hours. If you know you are allergic to bee stings, before leaving town be sure to consult your doctor about any medication you may need to take along. This is a good item to keep in your first-aid kit.

A honey bee leaves its stinger imbedded in the skin. It's best to remove the stinger with tweezers or by scraping with a fingernail. Wash the sting area with soap and water and apply ice or flush with cold water to reduce swelling and pain. Calamine lotion is available over-the-counter in drugstores. Baking soda works well by mixing with water to form a paste. (Baking soda is another good item for your first-aid kit.)

• Think ahead and plan ahead in order to be prepared for emergencies. When taking various foods on picnics, remember to keep the perishable items in coolers with lots of ice. Any food item containing mayonnaise is likely to go bad quickly. Don't let any food items sit in the hot sun. Eggs and uncooked meats need to be kept especially well-cooled.

• Take a car emergency kit. Some very good kits are available at auto parts stores. Or you can make up your own kit consisting of: flares, jumper cables, "HELP" sign, "CALL POLICE" sign, fire extinguisher, nylon rope, towel, flashlight, fuses, and an approved empty gasoline can. All of these can be put together in a plastic dishpan, which can also be used to carry water in an emergency.

• Buy and use a "Hide-A-Key" box. After the first time I locked my keys inside my car, the time I lost and the stress I endured sent me directly to a store to find a "Hide-A-Key" case and attach it to the car in a hidden place. (This makes an especially good gift for teen drivers.) For some reason keys locked inside a car cause lots of trouble to lots of people. So think ahead and prevent this kind of trouble!

Fall
Family
Organization

Don't act thoughtlessly, but try to
find out and do whatever the Lord
wants you to.
—*Ephesians 5:17*

*I*S GETTING the children organized a
problem for you after a summer of
irregular schedules? Here are a few steps to help you!

Step 1

Plan a back-to-school organizational day with each child. For the
working moms it may need to be a Saturday or an evening.

Step 2

With a child, go through his or her drawers and closets and throw
or give away summer clothing and outgrown shoes. A lot of the
summer clothing can be stored away for next summer. Put clothing
in boxes and label the boxes according to size, so when next summer
arrives, the clothing can be given to other members of the family or
to friends whom they will fit. That way you can recycle the children's
perfectly good clothes. The boxes can be stored in the basement,
garage, attic, or closets.

WARDROBE INVENTORY

Blouses	Pants	Skirts	Jackets	Sweaters

Dresses	Gowns	Lingerie	Shoes	Jewelry

Figure 1

Step 3

Take a wardrobe inventory! A checklist chart (Figure 1, page 60) like the one on the previous page will be helpful.

Step 4

Now comes the fun. Plan a time alone with each child to go over the inventory chart and to discuss needed new clothing to fill in the chart.

For moms that sew, take the child with you when picking out patterns and fabrics. If shopping from mail order catalogs, sit down and discuss the purchases with your child. Make it a togetherness time, and then he or she will feel part of the new wardrobe and the "I hate to wear that" syndrome will be eliminated. This method also teaches your children how to make decisions responsibly. Later on you'll find this guidance and time pay off as your children grow older and shop capably for themselves.

Step 5

Plan a family meeting to discuss home responsibilities. Make up a "Daily Work Planner Chart" (see Figure 2, page 62). Notice that mom's and dad's names are also listed on the chart. This shows that you work together as a family. Especially if mom is working outside the home, the family needs to support her all they can.

Step 6

Make a list of jobs the family can do to help around the house. (See Figure 3, page 63 with suggested jobs.) Put each item on a separate piece of paper and put each into a basket. You may need two baskets, one for children's jobs 3-7 years old and one for children 8-18. Then once a week the children will draw out two to five jobs. These jobs are put on the "Work Planner Chart."

As the children do their job, a happy face can be drawn by their name (or a sad face if they dropped the ball and neglected to do their job.) Stickers or stars can also be used. This makes for a colorful chart.

If they complete their jobs easily, they may draw another job from the basket and get extra credit or double stickers, stars, or happy faces. Children become excited about duties around the house and work toward a colorful chart for each week of the month.

DAILY WORK PLANNER CHART

Day of the Week	Mom	Dad	#1 Child	#2 Child	#3 Child	#4 Child	#5 Child
Saturday							
Sunday							
Monday							
Tuesday							
Wednesday							
Thursday							
Friday							

DAILY WORK PLANNER CHART

Day of the Week	Mom	Dad	#1 Child	#2 Child	#3 Child	#4 Child	#5 Child
Saturday	Clean House	Clean Garage	Bathe Dog	Mow Lawn	Clean Refrigerator		
Sunday	Plan Upcoming Week	Plan Upcoming Week	Set and Clear Table	Do Evening Dishes	Do Evening Dishes		
Monday	Menu Planning Grocery Shopping	Pick Up Dry Cleaning	Do Evening Dishes	Set and Clear Table	Empty Garbage Feed Dog		
Tuesday	Wash Clothes	Pick Up Rooms (clutter)	Fold and Distribute Clothes	Do Evening Dishes Feed Dog	Set and Clear Table		
Wednesday	Mop Floors	Clean Bathroom(s)	Set and Clear Table	Iron Clothes	Do Evening Dishes Feed Dog		
Thursday	Shopping Drop off Dry cleaning	Vacuum	Do Evening Dishes Feed Dog	Set and Clear Table	Empty Garbage		
Friday	Change Bed Linens	Water Plants	Dust Furniture	Do Evening Dishes Feed Dog	Set and Clear Table		

Figure 3

At the end of the month you can plan a special family surprise as a reward for jobs well done. You might say, "This month we've worked together as a family. Now we're going to play together as a family." Plan a fun Saturday bike ride ending with a picnic lunch, or a Friday evening by the fire popping corn and playing a favorite family game.

Organizing for fall can be a creative and productive time in your homes. Let's begin.

• Wallpaper scraps. It's always a good idea to save wallpaper scraps in case sections of the paper need to be repaired later. To make a patch, tear (don't cut) a scrap into the approximate size and shape needed. The irregular torn edges will blend better with the paper already on the wall, making the patch less apparent than it would be if cut.

• Paint splatters. Here's an easy way to erase paint splatters from a brick fireplace. Get a broken brick the same color as the brick on the fireplace and scrub it back and forth over the spattered areas. Brick against brick will abrade away most of the paint. Any remaining paint will pick up the brick color and thus be camouflaged.

• Turning one pound of butter into two pounds with gelatin. Let the butter stand at room temperature until soft. Into $1^1/4$ cup cold milk, soften one envelope of unflavored gelatin. Add $1^3/4$ cups hot milk; stir until gelatin is dissolved. Cool until lukewarm. Whip into butter with electric mixer. Keep covered in refrigerator. Use within one week as a spread, not for baking.

• Clutter. Work better and faster by tossing out things that are no longer needed or have lost their usefulness, such as stacks of old magazines or receipts. If you don't want to throw them out, store them in a box.

• Unfinished work. Don't let work pile up. Decide which projects need to be completed.

• Lots of choices. Since your time is limited, choose to do things that you enjoy or find useful. Don't overload yourself with tasks or responsibilities. Always strive to simplify your life.

• Procrastination. Do the jobs you dislike *first*. Once you've got those unpleasant tasks out of your way, you'll find that the rest of the work will be somewhat easier.

• Racing through each day. Try to work smarter, not harder. Plan your day. Pace your energy and skills through the day like a disciplined athlete getting ready for the Olympics. At the end of the day you will have achieved more and won't feel so tired and stressed.

• Cleaning the grout. To clean the grout between the tiles in your kitchen or bathroom, mix up a paste of scouring powder and hydrogen peroxide (just enough to make a paste.) Apply with an old toothbrush, let sit 20 minutes, then wash off with hot water and a scrub brush. (Keep the windows open as you work!) Try a mildew stain remover you can buy in the hardware store or supermarket and apply according to the directions on the container.

• Whitening a porcelain sink. First fill the sink with two or three inches of warm water. Add detergent and half a cup of chlorine bleach. Let sit 15 minutes, then wash the entire sink with the solution. Rinse thoroughly with hot tapwater.

• Cleaning glass or plastic shower stall doors. Just put a little lemon oil furniture polish on a soft clean cloth and rub the doors clean. Be careful not to get any of the lemon oil polish on your tiles. (The whole problem of keeping the shower stall doors clean can be avoided if everyone wipes the doors dry after taking a shower!)

• Speeding up a sluggish drain. First run hot tapwater down the drain, then pour in three tablespoons of baking soda and half a cup of distilled white vinegar. Stop up the drain and wait 15 minutes. The baking soda and vinegar will foam up, reacting with each other and eating away at whatever is slowing the drain. Finally, flush the drain with hot tapwater.

• Removing candle wax from a tablecloth. Place the waxy section of the tablecloth between two thicknesses of paper toweling and press with a warm iron. If a greasy spot remains, treat it with a dry cleaning fluid.

• Removing candle wax from a candlestick. Try pouring boiling water into the candlestick socket to melt the wax. Once melted it will wipe out easily.

• Getting white rings off furniture. Dampen a cloth with a small amount of mineral oil and dab it in fireplace ashes. Wipe gently on the ring, then polish or wax the wood as usual.

• Eliminating cooking odors. Boil 1 tablespoon white vinegar in 1 cup water over stove. This will eliminate unpleasant cooking odors.

• Eliminating tobacco odors. During and after a party, place a small bowl of white vinegar in the room.

• Freshening laundry. Add ⅓ cup baking soda to wash or rinse cycle. Clothes will be sweeter and cleaner smelling.

• Removing water spots from fabrics. Sponge entire stained area with white vinegar; let stand a few minutes. Rinse with clear, cool water and let dry.

• Removing lipstick, liquid makeup, or mascara from fabrics. Soak in dry-cleaning solution and let dry. Rinse and then wash.

• Freshening lunch boxes. Dampen a piece of fresh bread with white vinegar and put it in the lunchbox overnight.

• Making your blankets fluffier. Add 2 cups white vinegar to a washer tub of rinse water.

• Removing dark or burned stains from an electric iron. Rub with equal amounts of white or cider vinegar and salt, heated first in a small aluminum pan. Polish in the same way you do silver.

• Removing decals. Paint them with several coats of white vinegar. Give the vinegar time to soak in. After several minutes the decals should wash off easily.

• Deodorizing refrigerator. Place one opened box of baking soda in the back of the refrigerator or in a shelf on the door. Change every other month.

• Freshening drains and garbage disposal. Use a discarded box of baking soda previously used in your refrigerator.

• Removing burned or baked on foods from your cookware. Scrub with baking soda sprinkled on a plastic scouring pad; rinse and dry. You might also try warm soda paste soaked on burned area; keep wet, then scrub as needed.

• Deodorizing your carpet. Sprinkle dry baking soda on the rug. Allow to set overnight, then vacuum. (Test for color fastness in an inconspicuous area.)

• Deodorizing cat litter. Cover the bottom of the litter pan with 1 part baking soda; then cover baking soda with 3 parts litter to absorb odors for up to a week. Litter won't need replacing as often.

• Disinfecting wood chopping surfaces. Scrub with a mild bleach solution, then rinse and rub it with a thin coat of mineral or salad oil.

17

Year 'Round Clothing Care

She looks for wool and flax, and
works with her hands in delight.
—*Proverbs 31:13 NASB*

*W*ITH THE COST of clothing and fabrics these days, we need to know what we can do to keep our clothing fresh and new, especially if we are spending money on fairly expensive clothing.

We live only one hour from the Los Angeles garment district, and 90 percent of all my clothing is bought from 40 to 70 percent off. I don't have time to shop very often, so I need to take especially good care of my clothing so it will look new and fresh for several years. Here are some fun ideas and tips to do just that.

First of all I start with three basic items in a solid color:

1. A blazer or jacket
2. A skirt
3. Pants

To these three basics I then add blouses in prints or solid colors that will coordinate. Next I add a few sweaters and several accessories, such as scarves, ribbon ties, boots, jewelry, and perhaps a silk flower. Finally I purchase two pairs of shoes, one for casual wear and one pair for dress (the church type).

Since I do a great deal of traveling, I take these six to nine items and a few accessories (plus one all-weather coat) and coordinate them into approximately 12 to 16 outfits that will last 7 to 14 days.

How to Make Clothing Last

1. Dry clean your garments every eight to ten wearings (or longer if possible). Dry cleaning is hard on fabrics.

2. Rotate your various items of clothing as much as possible so they can regain their shape. I have a friend who rotates her garments by hanging them after each wearing at the right end of the closet. The next day she picks the skirt or pants that are on the left end of the closet. That way she knows how often they are worn. This works especially well with men's suits.

3. As soon as you take off your garments, empty the pockets, shake the garment well, and hang up immediately.

4. Have you ever thought of Scotchguarding your new fabrics? It's very effective and will last until the garment is cleaned or washed. (Then just spray it again.) You can also use Scotchguard on your fabric shoes.

5. Mend your garments as soon as they are damaged. Sew on those buttons and repair those rips and loose hems. My Bob has a tendency to tear out the seat of his pants, so I triple-stitch and zigzag the seams when they are new, even before they are worn. That keeps embarrassing moments to a minimum.

6. Keep from snagging your hose by using hand lotion to soften your hands before putting your hose on.

7. Hang wrinkled clothes in the bathroom while showering. The steam will cause the wrinkles to come out.

8. Let perfumes and deodorants dry on your body before getting dressed in order to prevent garment damage.

9. I put a scarf over my head before pulling a garment over my head to prevent a messed hairdo and makeup smudges and stains.

10. Hang blazers and coats on padded hangers to avoid hanger marks.

11. Keep sweaters in a drawer or shelf rather than on a hanger (to prevent stretching).

12. Skirts and pants are best hung on hangers with clips; or you can use clothespins on wire hangers.

13. Even very good jewelry can discolor your clothing, so just dab the backs with clear nail polish. The polish can also be painted on jewelry with rough edges that could pull fibers of fabrics.

14. Some stickpins can make holes in delicate fabrics, so be careful and don't wear them if you are in doubt.

15. Be sure to have your good leather shoes polished to retain their shine. It also feeds and preserves the leather.

16. Brush suede shoes with a suede brush that brings up the nap. You can use a nail file to rub off any little spots.

17. Replace heels and soles on your shoes before they wear down completely.

18. If your shoes get wet, stuff them with paper towels or newspaper and allow to dry away from direct heat.

19. Shoe trees are great to keep the shape in your shoes.

20. When storing leather handbags or shoes, never put them into plastic bags, since this can cause the leather to dry out. Instead, use fabric shoe bags or wrap the shoes in tissue and put them into shoeboxes.

21 Washday Hints to Relieve Laundry Stress

> She makes coverings for herself;
> her clothing is fine linen and
> purple.
> —*Proverbs 31:22* NASB

*D*OES WASHDAY come when there is nothing clean left to wear? Does your clothing need to be ironed before you can go out of the house, or do you go anyway looking wrinkled or crumpled? Do your children dash madly about in search of matching socks but are not able to find them because your washing machine ate them up or they fall out of a fitted sheet two weeks later, after you've thrown out the single one?

Sorting laundry can save time, stress, and energy. Children can be taught simple organizational techniques to save the family washday stress.

1. Divide your laundry into three cloth bags. These can be made from fabric or three large king-size pillowcases with a drawstring. Bag 1 is white for the soiled white clothes. Bag 2 is dark (brown, navy, black) for the dark soiled clothes (jeans, washcloths, etc.) Bag 3 is multicolored for the mixed-colored clothes. Colored plastic trash cans can also be used. Label the cans "colored," "white," and "dark." Show all members of the family how to sort their own dirty clothes by putting them in the proper bags or cans. Each child or

bedroom could have its own laundry bag. From there they take the clothes to the central sorting area, then sort their own into the three bags. (Or each day *all* dirty clothing goes to the sorting area.) On washdays or whenever the bags become full it's a simple matter of dumping bag 1 into the machine and swish, swash, the wash is done. To solve your missing-sock problem, invest in plastic sock sorters. These can be found in drug or variety stores. Safety pins are also great to keep socks paired during the wash and dry cycles. One mom purchased only white socks for the children, one size fits all. Remember, it's not what you *expect* but what you *inspect*. So be sure to teach the method and then inspect from time to time to see if they are doing it properly. Whatever goes *in* the bags inside out will come *out* inside out.

2. Each family member can also have his or her own bright-colored bin for clean folded clothes. Christine's is pink, Chad's is blue, Bevan's is white, mom's is red, and dad's is green. Or you can use all white bins (or dishpan-type bins) and color-code them with stick-on dots or colored felt markers with each family member's name on them.

3. Whoever folds the clothes places each person's items in his or her proper bin. It is then the responsibility of each family member to take his own bin to the drawers and empty the bin. Should the bin not return to the folding area, no clothes will be folded for that person.

4. Plan your washing days and start washing early in the day.

5. On washing day use cold water if possible, especially on colored clothes, as this will help them to stay bright longer.

6. Wash full loads rather than small ones. This saves energy and your appliances as well.

7. Never leave the washer or dryer running when you aren't home. A machine leak or short circuit can cause damage or, worse yet, start a fire.

8. If using a dryer, remove the clothes as soon as it stops, then hang and fold. This will save wrinkled items and many times save ironing items.

9. Forgot to take out the clothes in the dryer? Simply throw in a damp towel or washcloth and turn on the dryer again for five to ten minutes. The dampness from the towel will freshen the load and remove any wrinkles.

10. Hang as many clothes as possible on hangers, especially permanent-press garments. This will also help cut down on ironing. Put up a few hooks near the laundry area or string an indoor clothesline.

11. I recommend using plastic-colored hangers rather than metal ones. They prevent marks and creases on your garments. Using colored hangers can also color-code your family. Assign each person a different color. Then when you take the clothing out of the dryer, hang it on the appropriate-colored hanger: mom, white; dad, brown; Kevin, blue; Susie, yellow; etc.

12. Schedule at least one day a week for ironing, or three 15-minute slots per week. Keep ahead of your ironing; this will relieve your stress level and eliminate having to iron at the last minute before you leave the house.

13. To help ironing time go quickly, pray for the person whose clothing you are ironing. This way ironing can become a real joy and blessing.

14. Label your linen closet shelves so that whoever puts the sheets and towels away will know just the right spot for them. This prevents confusion, keeps your closet looking neat, and saves time in finding king-size or twin-size.

15. When your iron sticks, sprinkle a little salt onto a piece of waxed paper and run the hot iron over it. Rough, sticky spots will disappear as if by magic.

16. Always wash your throw rugs in cool or lukewarm water. (Hot water will cause the rubber backing to peel.) Let the rug dry on a line instead of in the dryer. You can fluff it up when it is dry in the no-heat cycle of your dryer.

17. Here's a little trick to make ironing easier: Using pieces of wax candles in an old cotton sock, swipe your iron every so often while ironing. The wax makes it glide smoothly, and your ironing goes faster.

18. Instead of using expensive fabric-softener sheets, pour one-fourth cup *white* vinegar in the last rinse of the washing cycle. This eliminates static cling, helps remove wrinkles, gives clothes a fresh smell by removing soap, and cleans the drains of the washer by removing soap scum and lint.

19. Another way to remove garment wrinkles: Hang wrinkled garments on the curtain rod in your bathroom and run very hot water from the shower. Close the bathroom door and let the water run for a couple of minutes. The steam will fade the wrinkles from your clothing. Great for those who travel!

20. If your steam iron clogs up, fill it with a mixture of one-fourth cup of vinegar and one cup of water and let it stand overnight. Heat the iron the next day. Remove the mixture and rinse with clear water.

Children

How to Get Your Children to Help Around the House

> Train up a child in the way he
> should go, and even when he is old
> he will not depart from it.
>
> —*Proverbs 22:6 NASB*

*A*S A MOTHER of five children under five years of age, at one time in my life it was easy to become overwhelmed and frustrated at trying to be Supermom. I needed help, and the help came from my family. I found a way to get my husband and children to help with the housework cheerfully. Even the toddlers helped.

Your children will benefit by one day becoming independent, responsible adults who are pleased with their accomplishments. So make the housework fun, give clearly defined directions, keep the jobs realistic, and avoid criticism. Above all, praise, praise, praise!

I wrote the jobs that they could do on individual pieces of paper and put them in a basket. Then they got to choose two or three jobs from that basket once a week. These jobs went onto a Work Planner Chart, which was posted. When jobs each day were completed they were marked with an "X" and a happy face or a sticker. By the end of the week the chart was full of marks; each child used a different-colored marking pen, and each loved to see his or her color appear often. Rewards came at the end of the week, with lots of praise!

Toddlers respond well to marks on a chart, and teens like to work on a point system. (So many points per job; add them up on Saturday and reward accordingly.) When our children got into junior high school, even their friends wanted their names on our Work Planner Chart. Why? Because we had a well-defined plan, we made it fun, and they were rewarded.

If you want your children to grow up believing that the mess belongs to the person who made it, don't teach them that they are helping mommy. Instead, applaud them for making *their* bed, dressing *themselves*, and putting *their* clothes away. Praise your children for keeping *their* room neat and putting *their* toys away. Thank them for doing a good job because they are such good workers. Help them to feel good about being a part of a family effort. Then they will learn that they are part of a family team in which each person contributes and each person appreciates the other.

Have the mindset that the child's room belongs to the child. Teach your children from an early age (one, two, three years old) to be responsible for their own clothes, bed, laundry, and toys. This way they will find out early that if they wish to live in a neat and clean room they will have to do the work themselves.

You ask, "What if they like to live in a mess?" You are still the winner because you are spared the time, energy, stress, and aggravation of doing it all.

At an early age, when they make their bed praise them for it! Praise will get you everywhere, and they'll want to do it again and again.

When they're ready to put away their toys, have boxes, bins, or low shelves available for them to use. Let them do it their own way, arranged by them and not you. Provide low hooks so they can hang their own sweaters, jammies, and jackets. Whenever possible, make a game of putting these things away.

One mom installed a wooden pole that went from the floor to the ceiling. Then she screwed cup hooks into the pole and sewed a plastic curtain ring onto each of the children's stuffed animals so the children could easily hang up their animals when they were finished with them. This arrangement also provided a creative decorator item, and the children loved hooking their teddy bears to the pole.

Make the chores fun and games. The children will want to work if you make it a happy time!

A toddler can set the table. Make a placemat out of paper and draw the shapes of the fork, plate, spoon, and glass. The child gets to put each item in it's proper place. Soon Susie or Timmy will want to set the table for everyone.

Let them play policeman or trashman. Give them a pillowcase to pickup toys, trash, and papers around the house and even in the yard.

Toddlers can feel important this way and can learn to like the feeling of work. Congratulations are in order for a job well done!

Help your child dress independently. Keep solid bottoms in a low drawer with printed tops. If you buy coordinates, any top will go with any bottom. Even a young child can choose what to wear within reason and limitations.

Avoid uncomfortable or difficult clothing. If you want to have children who can dress themselves, they certainly can't cope with tight collars or fancy buttons. Snaps and loose tops help them not to feel frustrated. The Velcro used on shoes today is great for little fingers and makes the children feel proud of themselves as they put on their own shoes.

Yes, children can learn to love to do their fair share around the house!

20

How to Teach Your Children About Money

Steady plodding brings prosperity;
hasty speculation brings poverty.
—*Proverbs 21:5*

$\mathcal{W}$E LIVE in a world where adults often find themselves in financial woes. Where do we learn about money? Usually by trial and error, since few families take the time to teach their children how to be smart with money. Yet at an early age, children should know about money and what it can do for them.

Children who learn about money at an early age will be ahead in this mystery game. Learning to deal with money properly will foster discipline, good work habits, and self-respect.

Here are eight ways in which you can help your children get a good handle on money.

1. **Start with an allowance.** Most experts advise that an allowance should not be tied directly to a child's daily chores. Children should help around the home not because they get paid for it but because they share responsibilities as members of a family. However, you might pay a child for doing *extra* jobs at home. This can develop his or her initiative. We know of parents who give stickers to their children when they do something that they haven't

specifically been asked to do. These stickers may then be redeemed for 25 cents each. This has been great for teaching not only initiative but also teamwork in the family.

An allowance is a vital tool for teaching children how to budget, save, and make their own decisions. Children learn from their mistakes when their own money has been lost or spent foolishly.

How large an allowance to give depends on your individual family status. It should be based on a fair budget that allows a reasonable amount for entertainment, snacks, lunch money, bus fare, and school supplies. Add some extra money to allow for church and savings. Be willing to hold your children responsible for living within their budget. Some weeks they may have to go without, particularly when they run out of money.

2. **Model the proper use of credit.** In today's society we see the results of individuals and couples using bad judgment regarding credit.

Explain to your children the conditions when it's necessary to use credit and the importance of paying their loan back on a timely basis. You can make this a great teaching tool. Give them practice in filling out credit forms. Their first loan might be from you to them for a special purchase. Go through all the mechanics that a bank would; have them fill out a credit application and sign a paper with all the information stated. Let them understand about interest, installment payments, balloon payments, late payment costs, etc. Teach them to be responsible to pay on time.

3. **Teach your children how to save**. In today's instant society it is hard to teach this lesson. At times we should deny our children certain material things so that they have a reason to save. As they get older they will want bicycles, stereos, a car, a big trip, etc. They need to learn the habit of saving so they can then buy these larger items.

One of the first ways to begin teaching the concept of saving is to give the children some form of piggy bank. Spare change or extra earnings can go into the piggy bank. When it gets full you might want to open an account at a local bank.

When your children are older you might want to establish a passbook account at a local bank so they can go to the bank and personally deposit money to their account. Most banks will not pay interest until the balance becomes larger, but at least this habit of depositing money will help your children begin thinking about saving.

In the end, children who learn how to save will better appreciate what they've worked to acquire.

4. Show them how to be wise in their spending. Take your children with you when you shop, and show them some cost comparisons. They will soon see that with a little effort they can save a lot of money. You might want to demonstrate this principle to them in a tangible way when they want to purchase a larger item for themselves. Go with them to several stores to look for that one item, writing down the highest price and the lowest price for that item. This way they can really see how much they can save by comparison shopping.

Clothing is an area where a lot of lessons on wise spending can be made. After awhile your children will realize that designer clothes cost a lot more just for that particular label or patch. Our daughter, Jenny, soon learned that outlet stores were great bargains for clothes dollars. To this day she can still find excellent bargains by comparison shopping.

5. Let them work part-time. There are many excellent part-time jobs waiting for your child. Fast-food outlets, markets, malls, babysitting, etc. can give valuable work experience to your children. Some entrepreneurial youngsters even begin a thriving business based on their skills and interest. These part-time jobs are real confidence boosters. Just remember to help your child keep a proper balance between work, home, church, and school. A limit of 10 to 15 hours per week might be a good guideline.

6. Let them help you with your budgeting. Encourage your children to help you budget for the family finances. This gives them experience in real-life money problems. They also get a better idea about your family's income and expenses. Children can have good suggestions about how to better utilize the family finances, and their experience can give them a better understanding of why your family can't afford certain luxuries.

7. Give them experience in handling adult expenses. As your children get older they need to experience real-life costs. Since children normally live at home, they don't always understand true-to-life expenses. Let them experience paying for their own telephone bill, car expenses, and clothing expenses. Depending upon the situation, having them pay a portion of the utility and household bills can be an invaluable experience for children who have left school and are still living at home.

8. Show them how to give to the Lord. At a very young stage in life, parents and children should talk about where things come from. The children should be aware that all things are given from God and that He is just letting us borrow them for a time. Children can understand that we are to return back to God what He has so abundantly given to us. This principle can be experienced through either Sunday school or their church offerings. When special projects at church come up, you might want to review these needs with your children so they can decide whether they want to give extra money above what they normally give to their church. Early training in this area provides a valuable basis for learning how to be a giver in life and not a taker.

Your children will learn about money from *you*, so be a good model. If you have good habits, they will reflect that; if you struggle with finances, so will they. One valuable lesson to teach them is that money doesn't reflect love. A hug, a smile, a kiss, or just time spent together is much more valuable than money.

Summertime Projects to Keep Your Children Busy

> Children are a gift from God; they are his reward.
> —*Psalm 127:3*

*O*NE JULY afternoon our Brad and Jenny echoed, "There's nothing to do, Mom. What can we do to have some fun?"

With a quick prayer and a lot of creativity we came up with our Summer Project Box. We scurried around the house to find just the right box. (The right box should be sturdy and made of cardboard. A shoebox, hatbox, or even a file-type box will do.) To keep our projects separate we made cardboard dividers (file folders will also do). On these dividers we listed summer projects which the children were interested in exploring. I found that they were very creative in their ideas.

Here are some of our projects that were successful. Your children may have other projects, depending upon their ages and interest.

Sports/Games

Set up a file on your favorite sports star. Include photos (you can send for them), articles from newspapers and magazines, and autographs.

Also include copies of letters which your children write to their favorite stars in football, baseball, hockey, skating, etc.

Organize a Summer Olympics in your neighborhood. Time the running events and relay races, and measure the long jumps. Design and create medals and/or rewards.

Set up a bowling alley in your backyard by using milk cartons for pins and a large rubber ball. Tell the children they can ask neighbors to save their milk cartons to contribute to this project.

Garden/Nature

Plant and care for a vegetable garden or flower garden. Children love to watch the plants come up and to eventually harvest the vegetables and pick the flowers. Keep records on plant growth, watering, and fertilizing.

Make a study of insects. Keep a record of what they eat and how they live. Make sketches of them. Take your children to the library and find books about insects and how to identify them.

Press wildflowers to use for art projects, Christmas cards, and/or thank-you notes.

Find rocks—smooth, round, and odd-shaped. Make creative items with them by painting them with flowers, people, and animals. One summer the children filled their wagons with the rocks they had painted and sold them door-to-door as paperweights.

Food

Set up a lemonade stand for the neighborhood. This is a great way for younger children to learn about running a small business. Have them make the posters, set the cost, and stock the stand with such items as lemonade, ice, and cups, and perhaps such additional items as muffins, cookies, licorice, and nuts. Garden vegetables could also be sold (corn, carrots, radishes, pumpkins, etc.).

Have your children choose a recipe and make something from scratch. Have them file a copy of the recipe in a box, with notes on how it came out.

Beach/Lake

Take pictures or make sketches of various kinds of boats. Collect shells and devise your own classification system. Take a field trip to the beach and discover the tidepools. List the different kinds of crabs, snails, starfish, etc.

Go lake or ocean fishing and bring home the catch for dinner. Study nature, balances of life, tadpoles, and frogs.

Go sailing, canoeing, rowing. List the activity and what was learned. Put into the Project Box.

Vacations/Short Trips

Conduct research to find places in your area that would make good family trips. Write a short description of each place and include, if possible, a photo or drawing of the spot. Share your research with the family.

Make a file of activities for car, plane, train. List necessary items to take along. Include clothing, camera, etc. Collect maps, brochures, and postcards from your travels and file them in the Project Box.

The children may come up with more project categories to add to the Project Box. They will be excited by simply putting together their box. The summer will be fun, exciting, and a real learning time for your children as they choose a project on those days when they would otherwise say, "But, mom, there's nothing to do!"

Organizing Fun Ways for Your Children to Earn Money

Much is required from those to whom much is given, for their responsibility is greater.

—Luke 12:48

*T*O BE INDUSTRIOUS is what Proverbs 31 tells us women to strive to achieve. But do we teach that to our children? As our own children grew up, we thought of all kinds of ways to create money-earning ventures. One of the very first projects they did was at ages five and six. We lived in a beach area in Southern California and spent time collecting shells and rocks. We had so many that they overflowed the bedrooms. So one summer we had a rock-painting session in the garage with acrylic paints. The children made creative, colorful rocks and shells, and when they were finished they displayed their creations in their wagon, walking the neighborhood and selling their rocks and shells for five cents each. They were really excited to sell rocks and shells for cash!

It's hard for children to earn money by doing chores around the house. Even for money it just isn't the same as earning it independently. When children earn money for themselves it gives them a sense of responsibility. When the jobs are fun and helpful, everyone benefits.

How much should mom be involved? Plenty at first. Make sure you know the people who are hiring your child. Help match your child's age and ability to the job in question, and be sure the child is realistically paid for his or her time. After that pull back, relax, and watch your child blossom with the satisfaction of earning money for a job well done.

Over the years we came up with many moneymaking ideas. Here are some of the family-tested ones that WORK!

1. **Toy Sale.** This children's version of the garage sale works especially well when the prices are kept low, since most customers will be other children. Put pricetags on everything, post a sign at the bottom of the driveway, and place the most eye-catching items up front. Let the children take it from there. They will learn about making change, negotiating, and (after sitting for hours between customers) perseverance.

2. **Pet-sitting.** Many owners of birds, cats, and goldfish (and other pets that don't need walking) hire a sitter to come in every day to feed the animals, change what needs changing, and give the pets some love and affection. Depending on the child's age, you may have to help lock and unlock the pet owner's doors or gates. But once inside, it's the child's job, and it's a good one. Standard rates of pay for this service are between $1.50 and $4.00 per day.

3. **Yard Work.** Even before they're old enough to handle power equipment, children can help garden in other ways. Their young backs don't get nearly as tired from pulling weeds and planting flowers as adults' do, and children make great scouts for hidden rocks and branches that play havoc with the lawnmower. Rates should be a penny per rock for the tiny tots and more when the work is harder.

4. **Dog-Walking.** The size of the dog may dictate the size of the walker, but most kids can handle this job. People are surprisingly eager to pay someone else to walk their dog, especially when the weather is sloppy. Today's busy person is usually happy to pay $1.00 per walk.

5. **Assisting at Children's Birthday Parties.** The hired helper should be only a few years older than the party group. He can help pass out food, round up trash and wrapping paper, oversee the games, and provide a vital extra set of eyes and hands for those guests who wander off and search for something breakable. Rate of pay: $3.00 per party.

6. **Cleaning Out Crawl Spaces, Storage Sheds, Etc.** The more cramped the space, the better little bodies can help to clean it.

Children are surprisingly strong and endlessly curious about cluttered nooks and crannies. Though they can't sort through the things you've accumulated, it may be worth paying a few cents just for the company. Rate of pay: 50¢ per hour.

7. **Child-Walking.** An older child can walk a younger child to school every day, to a music lesson, or to the playground for a time of teeter-totter or swinging. Estimated rate of pay: 25¢ per day.

8. **Summer Stock.** This is always a fun time for children to express their talents. Plan a show where several children put on an act or talent show. Sing a song or lip sync to a record, tell a few jokes, play an instrument, juggle, write and then read a poem, do a dance, or teach the dog a trick and then have the dog do tricks. Sell tickets to the show. Suggested ticket price: 20¢ to 50¢ each, depending on the talents.

9. **Summer Camp.** This is great fun for several children to help in. Together they can supervise up to eight children—making crafts, running relay races, and conducting a story read-aloud hour.

Two hours is usually the maximum attention span for most children. Rates: from $2.00 to $4.00 per child, depending on the cost of necessary craft items, such as popsicle sticks, yarn, paints, cookies, juice, and other goodies.

10. **Car Wash.** Always a hit. Cloths, whisk broom, buckets, and window spray will be the equipment needed. Children can go door-to-door and make appointments. After the winter weather has thawed out and the spring rains are over is a good time to canvass the neighborhood. If they do a good job they could very well turn this into a weekly job. Rates range from $1.50 to $3.00 per car, depending on the size of the car and how well the job is completed.

11. **House-Sitting.** Many people like their home taken care of when out of town or on vacation. This is a good opportunity for the child to learn responsibility. The lawn and potted plants (indoor and outdoor) need watering, paper and mail taken inside, and lights turned on and off to make the situation seem normal. Pets can also be fed and watered. The rate of pay will depend on the amount of work done. Range: $1.00 to $5.00 per day.

Child Safety

*In everything you do, stay away
from complaining and arguing.*
—Philippians 2:14

*C*HARCOAL lighter fluid may not taste
good, but a thirsty child may easily grab a
can, put it to his mouth, and down a swallow in a matter of seconds.

I was reminded of this type of household accident (and others)
shortly after our three grandchildren were born. I realized once
again the importance of making my home safe for small children.

Accidents happen when we least expect them, and they are most
common within our own homes. The National Safety Council estimates that there is a home accident every seven seconds.

Even if you don't have children, making your home safe for
visitors with small children is very important.

I've compiled a list to help you get started.

Kitchen Safety

• Keep knives in a knife holder on a wall or in a higher drawer.
• Put knives in dishwasher point down.
• Store cleaning items in a plastic bucket or a carry-all with a
handle. Place it on a shelf in the garage or the hall closet.

The bucket or carry-all can then be taken from room to room for cleaning and will free up the space under the kitchen sink for storing paper towels, napkins, paper plates, and cups.

• When cooking on your kitchen range, keep the handles of your pots turned *away* from the front of the stove. If you don't do this, children can easily dump a pot of boiling water or food on their heads by pulling on a handle or swinging a toy overhead.

• Always wrap broken glass in paper or place it in an old paper bag before throwing it into the trash. This goes for razor blades and jagged metal lids as well. A child may drop a toy into the trash and try to retrieve it, or may be taking out the trash and see an item he wants to look at or take out.

• When wiping up broken glass off the floor, use a dampened paper towel. This will ensure that you get all the pieces and will also protect your hands.

• Teach your children how to pour hot water slowly and to aim steam away from them so it doesn't gush out and burn them. Be sure to check the lid of a teapot or kettle to see that it fits tightly and won't fall into the cup and splash boiling hot water all over.

• Any poisons or extremely dangerous products should be kept in a locked cabinet on a very high shelf.

• Never store products in unlabeled jars or cans. It's just too easy to forget what's inside.

• For all electrical outlets, purchase cover caps for your child's safety. The caps are very inexpensive and can be purchased at drugstores, hardware stores and even children's shops.

• Never leave a cord plugged into a socket with the other end exposed for a child to put into his mouth. Use an empty toilet paper tube to wrap your cords around, and place the tube in a safe drawer.

Bathroom Safety

• Never leave children in the bathtub unattended; a lifeguard needs to be on duty at all times. Falling is just one of the hazards that younger children face in the tub. Don't answer the door or telephone without taking the child with you.

• Check the water temperature carefully before putting children in the tub or shower. It can start out warm but then get really hot if you accidentally brush the faucet handle with your hand. Never allow children to fiddle with the faucets. Scalds can happen very quickly.

• Never add hot water to the bathtub when the baby is in it. Be sure the hot water faucet is turned off tightly. Wrap a washcloth around the faucet for safety when the child is in the tub.

• Tell the whole family that shower valves should be turned to "OFF" after use. Otherwise a bather or bathtub cleaner may get scalding water on his or her head.

• Store all medications in a cool, dry place somewhere other than the bathroom. This way there is no danger of little hands reaching your medicine, and it will not be damaged by moisture.

Door Safety

• If you have small children in your home, keep your bathroom doors closed at all times. A latch placed up high where toddlers can't unlatch it should do the trick.

• Be careful of bathroom doors that lock from the inside. Be sure you have an emergency key that will open the door from the outside should junior become locked in and you locked out.

• Door gates can be used across bathroom or bedroom doors, stairs, and many other places that you want to keep away from children. These gates can be purchased in most stores that have baby departments. Look for them also at garage sales or in want ads in newspapers.

Miscellaneous Safety

• Post emergency phone numbers near your phone for both yourself and babysitters.

• Take a first-aid class that includes CPR (mouth-to-mouth resuscitation) at your local Red Cross chapter.

• Give your children swimming lessons at a very early age and/or teach them in the bathtub how to hold their breath underwater. Many community pools offer swimming lessons.

• If you don't already have a first-aid kit, get one or make up your own. Store it out of children's reach.

• Use side rails on small children's beds to keep infants from falling out. These can be purchased out of catalogs or in children's departments at most stores.

• Keep scissors, plastic bags, icepicks, and matches away from the reach of children.

• Warn children not to touch an electrical appliance plug with wet hands.

Remember, safety saves lives!

Preparing for Vacation Travel

If you refuse to discipline your son,
it proves you don't love him; for if
you love him you will be prompt to
punish him.

—*Proverbs 13:24*

*B*ELIEVE IT or not, it can be a joy to travel with your children!

Granted, the preparation for a trip sometimes seems exhausting, and you may wonder if it is worth it all to leave the house, the pets, and a regular routine. But the excitement and wonder of children as they experience new sights will truly be ample reward for the effort involved.

Here are some hints for making your trip smoother for the whole family.

• **Prepare your child for the exciting adventure.** Talk with them about where you are going and what you will be doing. As a child grows out of the infant and toddler stages and as his world expands to include friends, some verbal preparation becomes very important.

Tell your youngsters about the fun that is in store for them. Show them books, maps, and photographs about your route and destination. Be sure to reassure them that you will soon return home and that the toys they didn't take with them will still be there when they get back.

• **Watch your tendency to overpack.** The rule of thumb for experienced travelers applies to children as well: *Take just what you need and no more.*

The length of the trip (adjusted for the dirt factor for your children) should give you a reasonable handle on the amount of clothing they will need each day. Bear in mind that a public laundromat will probably be available during your travels.

• **Pack only clothing that your children like.** Let them help you pack. Even a three-year old can learn to help. Lay out five items and let them choose two to take along. This is a great teaching tool.

In our family, our children eventually did all their own packing. I merely checked their items to be sure all the bases were covered. Sometimes we had to leave items behind because, as time and experience taught us, we learned we were wearing only half of what we took. However, always take a sweater or sweatshirt, since temperatures can sometimes change very quickly, even in tropical areas.

• **Take toys that your children enjoy.** Again, let your child help in this area. A toy that you consider mundane might provide considerable amusement to your child.

It's also a good idea to stash away a couple of new attention-getters—maybe a special surprise like a new toy that he or she has always wanted. But don't forget the tried and true, either. A special pillow, favorite blanket, cuddly stuffed teddy, or special doll are often comforting for a child sleeping in a strange bed for the first time.

• **Consider a backpack for the preschooler and older child.** This is a great way of limiting items or toys taken. Make a rule that your children can take along whatever fits into their backpack.

• **Bring along a surprise box**. Children love it when mom and dad have secrets for them. Your box can include such items as toys, food snacks, puzzles, books, and word games. Be creative but keep it a surprise, and when things get hectic or a child gets irritable, pull out the surprise box.

• **Remember car seats**. If you are renting a car for your trip, request a car seat for any child four years old and younger. Many rental agencies provide these seats, but the availability is sometimes limited, so it is important to reserve one.

• **Plan frequent stops.** This is very important if you are traveling by car with small children. Cramped legs and fidgety children will be the cause of many arguments if not taken care of sensibly.

Give your children plenty of opportunities to get out and run, skip, and jump for a few minutes, and also to use the restroom.

• **Always carry a small cooler with you.** Keep a cooler filled with milk, fruit juice, snacks, and fruit. This will be a pick-me-up, and the refreshment is always welcome. It will also prevent too many fast-food stops. Picnic whenever possible; it's cheaper and children love it.

• **Invest in a first-aid kit.** Fill an empty coffee can with Band-Aids, children's aspirin, antiseptic, thermometer, scissors, safety pins, tweezers, adhesive tape, gauze, and cotton balls. Try to cover all bases. Don't forget a good supply of handy wipes and a blanket.

• **Bring a flashlight.** Be sure to check the batteries before leaving home. When all else fails, children love to play with a flashlight. Take along an extra set of batteries.

• **Throw in your bathing suits**. Keep these in an easy-to-get-to place. Many motels and hotels have pools that are usable even in the winter months. They may also have hot tubs or Jacuzzis. Also, you may find yourself stopping by a lake or beach for a quick swim.

• **Give your children their own map.** Depending on the age of your children, give them a map so they can follow the route and tell you how far it is to the next stop or town. Older children can also keep a journal of the trip.

• **Send up a prayer for safety and patience.** Before we drive out of our driveway, we always offer a prayer for protection and patience. Prayer during the trips also helps to calm a tense situation.

Some of your most memorable times together as a family will come from traveling on vacation. With a little planning and preparation, those memories can be truly happy ones.

Off to School

Let the little children come to Me,
and do not forbid them, for of such
is the kingdom of God.

—*Mark 10:14* NKJV

I CAN vividly remember when my niece, Keri, was living with us. We had done everything possible to make sure that she knew how to walk to school on that first day of kindergarten. We had even made dry runs, with her walking without us and us following behind in a car to make sure she got there. And in practice she did well.

On that first morning to school she left the house all dressed with new clothes, little knapsack, and a lunchbox. We were so excited on that first day of school. We kissed her goodbye, took a picture, and said goodbye. Off she walked in the direction of her new school. But in about 30 minutes the principal of the adjoining elementary school called and said, "Your niece Keri is here at the wrong school!"

No matter how hard we try, our efforts sometimes go unnoticed. However, there are certain steps we can take to make sure that the first school experience is at least somewhat successful.

Walk with your child to school or the bus stop at least once before the school year starts. Be sure the child understands any special arrangements you have made for his or her going to school and returning home. Practice the proper way to cross the street at every opportunity.

Be sure your child has seen and used a public toilet (including a urinal for boys) so that the school restrooms won't seem strange. Teach your children to use the correct words to ask to "go to the restroom or toilet." Emphasize the need to wash hands even when grownups are not around with reminders.

If your child will be eating lunch in the school cafeteria, take him or her to eat at a cafeteria-style restaurant, so that the procedures will be familiar. Let your child practice at home carrying a loaded food tray or using a lunchbox. Remind him or her to bring his lunchbox home each day.

It is very important for your child to know his or her full name, address, and home and work telephone numbers. (At least Keri did know how to get in touch with me.) An excellent way to teach these numbers is to set them to the tune of a nursery rhyme or a popular song. Be sure to give the school office your *work* number as well as your home number, plus the name and number of a parent substitute to call if you're not available in an emergency.

Make a safe place to keep any notes "to" and "from" the teacher. I inserted a manila envelope with holes punched on one side into my child's loose-leaf notebook. This way the notes to home didn't fall out and get lost.

Sick Days

Is your child too sick to go to school? This is a common cry heard by mom and dad. Talk to your child and carefully listen to what he or she is saying. The problem may not be stated in words but instead may be hidden beneath several unrelated answers. If you decide to allow your child to stay home from school, have a quiet talk showing a lot of love from mom.

If your child has too many pleas for sick days, consider causes other than illness, such as being teased, or frightened, fear of parental separation, etc. If you choose to keep your child home from school and in your judgment the child is not truly ill, staying home should not be a fun time. Put the child to bed for the day to "get well." If his pleas continue, make an appointment with your family doctor and your child's teachers. Both professionals might give you valuable feedback to why your child wants to stay home.

Reasons to Keep a Child Home From School

- A fever of 101 degrees or greater.
- Nausea and/or vomiting.
- Abdominal cramps.
- Diarrhea.
- A cold, when it is associated with a fever, frequent coughing, or heavy nasal congestion.
- A cough, when its symptoms aren't due to any allergy or the aftereffects of a recent illness.
- A sore throat, with fever.
- Any unidentified rash. This should be checked promptly by your doctor for the possibility of measles, chicken pox, or other infectious disease.
- Any infectious disease that your doctor has diagnosed.
- An earache.
- Conjunctivitis (pinkeye).
- Your own visual test or gut feeling that tells you your child really isn't well.
- Your child is overly tired or emotional.

Send your child off to school with a hug and a smile!

Finances

26

Keeping Your Utility Bills Down

My health fails; my spirits droop,
yet God remains. He is the strength
of my heart; he is mine forever!

—Psalm 73:26

*E*NERGY BILLS are never fun to pay. Although some factors may be beyond your control (extreme weather conditions, home location, or illness in the family), there are ways to make your use of energy more efficient and to reduce your energy bills. Here are some tips and ideas to help stabilize those bills.

Heating

Your heating system is probably your home's biggest energy user in the winter. It can be an energy waster if you don't use it wisely.

1. Leave the thermostat alone. During the day set it at 65 degrees or below. You raise operating costs 5 percent every time you raise the thermostat two degrees. Turn it down to 55 degrees or off at bedtime for more energy savings.

2. Proper insulation keeps your home warm in winter and cool in summer. In fact, up to 20 percent of your heating energy can be lost through an uninsulated ceiling.

3. Cut more heat loss by weatherstripping doors and windows. Close the damper when not using the fireplace or else heat will escape. Close off rooms not in use, along with heating vents, though not in more than 30 percent of the house. (Make sure you leave the vent open nearest the thermostat to insure proper temperature sensing.) Turn off individual thermostats.

4. Close draperies at night to keep out the cold. Open them during the day to let the sun shine through.

Lighting

Although individual lights don't use much energy, because houses are full of them and they get so much use (especially in winter), lighting costs can add up. Here are some ideas on keeping lighting costs down.

1. Fluorescent lights provide three times the light for the same amount of electricity as incandescent lights. They are very economical for bathrooms and kitchens, last ten times as long as incandescent bulbs, and produce less wasted heat.

2. Dimmer switches can multiply bulb life up to 12 times while they reduce electricity use.

3. Turn lights off when you're leaving a room and advise your family to do the same.

4. Let the light shine through. Lampshades lined in white give the best light. Tall, narrow shades or short, dark-colored ones waste watts. (Dirt and dust absorb light too, so add bulb-dusting to your cleaning list.)

5. One properly situated light in a room will do the work of three or four carelessly placed fixtures. Rearrange your room so the light is used more efficiently. If you're redecorating, use light colors. Dark colors absorb light.

6. Don't use infrared heating lights for night lights or general lighting.

7. Use lower-watt bulbs.

8. Turn off all outdoor lights except those necessary for safety and security.

Hot Water

Although hot water is the third-largest energy user in the average household, its use can be cut down painlessly.

1. Consider flow-restricting devices. These devices can cut water consumption in half.

2. Buy a water heater insulation blanket. This saves up to 9 percent of your water heater costs.

3. Fix the drips on all faucets. One drip a second can waste up to 700 gallons of hot water a year!

4. Take showers instead of baths. The shower's the winner for less hot water use if you keep your shower time under five minutes. (If you need to wash your hair, do it in the sink. A shower just to shampoo is a hot water waster.)

5. Monitor the use of the dishwasher. Run it once a day or less. It uses about 13 gallons each time instead of the 10 gallons each time you wash dishes by hand.

6. Use cold water for the garbage disposal. It solidifies the grease and flushes it away easily.

7. Turn down the temperature on your hot water heater to 140 degrees. (That's a "medium" setting if your dial isn't numbered.) If you don't have a dishwasher, 120 degrees may be adequate.

When you go away on vacation, set the pilot setting on "low" or turn it off altogether. If you have an electric water heater, it may be the type on which the upper thermostat can be set 10 degrees lower than the bottom one.

Energy-Saving Tips Around the Home

Always be joyful. Always keep on praying. No matter what happens, always be thankful, for this is God's will for you.

—1 Thessalonians 5:16-18

*I*T SOMETIMES seems surprising how those energy bills can jump around from month to month. What can you do to stabilize those bills and hold down the energy costs?

Some factors may be beyond your control: extreme weather, location of home, illness in family, old or less efficient appliances, etc. Additional houseguests, entertaining, building around the house, special projects, and vacations can often contribute to fluctuation in your energy usage.

Most energy users in the home are easily recognized, and many times you can make these more efficient. Here are some tips and ideas to help you stabilize those energy bills.

Refrigerator/Freezer

Your refrigerator/freezer is probably one of the biggest energy users in your home. Here are some ways to beat the cost of keeping things cool.

1. *Keep it clean.* In a manual-defrost model more than half an inch of frost can build up and make the appliance work harder, so *defrost regularly.* Vacuum clean the condenser coils below or at the back of the refrigerator/freezer three or four times a year. Clean coils keep it running efficiently and help save energy.

2. *Keep it closed.* The time for decisions is not when you have the door open. Get everything you need for a sandwich or recipe in one trip.

3. *Keep it full.* Frozen food helps keep the air cool in your freezer. But don't overpack food in either refrigerator or freezer, or the cold air won't have space to circulate properly.

4. *Heat has no business in the refrigerator.* Cool dishes before you store them so your appliance won't have to work so hard.

5. *Investigate before you buy.* A frost-free refrigerator/freezer may use 30 percent more electricity than a manual-defrost unit. Also, be sure to choose the correct cubic footage for your family, since a too-full or too-empty refrigerator/freezer wastes energy.

6. *Unplug your second refrigerator.* Refrigerators are big energy users, so if your second refrigerator is not being used to full capacity, unplug it. It could save you $15 a month or more, depending on its size.

Range/Oven

Your food budget shouldn't stop at the checkout counter. These days the cost of preparing the food can add up. Here are some tips on holding down cooking costs.

1. *Pots and pans are important.* Pans with flared sides or that are smaller than your burner let heat escape. If they're too big or have warped bottoms, food won't cook evenly. (For most foods, a medium-weight aluminum pan cooks fast and efficiently. Save your heavy pans for foods that require slow, steady cooking.)

2. *Cover up.* Use pan covers, since trapped steam cooks food quickly. Also, thaw foods completely before cooking.

3. *Preheating is out.* Unless you're baking things like breads and cakes, preheating isn't necessary and is very costly. Casseroles and broiled foods don't need it.

4. *Plan all-oven meals.* A meal like meat loaf, baked tomatoes, scalloped potatoes, and baked apples can all cook at the same time and temperature.

5. *Limit your boiling.* Water doesn't get any hotter with prolonged boiling. Therefore when you need to bring water to a boil

(e.g. for making drip coffee), turn off your range once the water has started to boil.

6. *Keep that oven door closed.* Every time you open the door, you lose 25 degrees of heat. Get yourself a timer and just be patient.

7. *Use your free heat.* A gas oven retains heat for up to 15 minutes, an electric oven for up to half an hour, and an electric range-top element for three to five minutes. Use that free heat to warm up desserts or rolls or to freshen crackers and cookies.

8. *Keep it clean.* A range free of grease and baked-on residue works better and costs you less.

9. *Use a microwave oven.* A microwave oven uses about the same amount of energy per hour as a conventional electric oven but cooks most foods in less than half the time. This can mean big savings on the cooking portion of your bill.

10. *Use your electric skillet.* Use your broiler oven or toaster oven instead of your electric range's oven for cooking and baking in small quantities. These can use as little as half the energy and won't heat up the kitchen nearly as much.

Washer/Dryer

Here's how to get the most out of that costly hot water.

1. *Wash full loads.* Washing two or three large items (like sheets) with a number of small ones (but don't pack them in) will give you a clean wash without taxing your washer's motor. If it is necessary to wash less than a full load, adjust the water-level settings accordingly.

2. *Sort by fabric, color, and degree of soil.* Use hot water only for whites, hard-to-clean items, and sterilizing. Use cold and warm water on all the rest. Your clothes will be just as clean, will fade less, and will have fewer wrinkles (which might save you some ironing).

3. *Check hose and faucet connections.* If the hose is cracked or the faucet connection is loose, you're probably losing hot water.

4. *Don't overkill.* Don't overdo it on soap, washing cycle, or drying. An oversudsed machine uses more energy. Regular clothes need only a 10- to 15-minute washing cycle. And overdrying will age your clothes and make them stiff and wrinkled.

5. *Get the lint out.* Clean the filters on the dryer after every use. Besides making your clothes more attractive, a lint-free machine works more efficiently.

6. *Use your clothesline.* It will save you 100 percent of the energy otherwise consumed by your gas or electric dryer. This could

amount to between $2 and $9 of the average $70 bill paid monthly in some areas of the country.

Small Appliances

Some small appliances can do the same jobs with half the energy use as their full-sized counterparts. Use them whenever practical.

1. *Use small appliances.* Small appliances use less energy if you remember to turn them off when you're through. Pull the plug on your coffeepot, iron, electric skillet, and curling iron. (A memory lapse will waste energy and might ruin the appliance.)

2. *Little appliances are okay.* You needn't be guilt-stricken about enjoying the luxury of an electric toothbrush or carving knife. (A continuous-charge toothbrush usually uses less than five cents a month and a carving knife less than ten cents a year.) Cut down instead on the *big* appliances. They're the ones that add up on your electric bill.

Air Conditioning

In many areas keeping cool in summer can cost a lot more than keeping warm in winter. Here are some things you can do to hold down the cost.

1. *Watch your degree of comfort.* Set your thermostat at 78 degrees or above. A setting of 78 instead of 73 saves 20 to 25 percent of your AC operating costs.

2. *Keep the cool air inside.* Close doors and windows. Check the weather-stripping. Seal up cracks. Insulate. These measures will help cut heating costs in the winter as well.

3. *Don't block vents.* Move furniture away from vents and window units. Trim shrubbery outside, too.

4. *Close drapes or blinds.* This helps keep the sun's heat out. Solar screens and shades can also effectively block a large amount of the sun's heat before it enters your home.

5. *Check your filters.* Do this once a month during cooling season. Vacuum or replace them as necessary.

6. *Grow deciduous trees.* Plant them where they will shade your house from the sun's hottest rays in the summer and let warming sun through in the winter.

7. *Check the EER before you buy.* Some systems use less energy than others—sometimes only half as much. Find the Energy Efficiency Rating (EER) on the yellow energy-guide label. The higher

the EER, the more efficient the unit. An EER of 10 will consume half the energy of a similar unit rated 5.

Swimming Pool

If you have a pool, a major portion of your energy outlay is the cost of operating it. Here are some ways to get control of swimming pool energy costs.

1. *Lower your pool's temperature.* Lowering your pool heater setting just two degrees can reduce your pool heating substantially. (A reduction from 80 degrees to 78 degrees could save up to 20 percent of heating costs.) The lower temperature saves on chemicals, too.

2. *Use a swimming pool cover.* You can save as much as 80 percent on your summer pool-heating bill by using a pool cover.

3. *Heat early in the morning.* The sun and the pool heater work together most efficiently during the morning hours.

4. *Protect your pool from wind.* Wind has the same effect on your pool as blowing on hot soup: It cools it. Hedges, fences, and cabanas help keep wind down.

5. *Don't overfilter.* Most pools require only four to five hours of filtering a day in summer and two to three hours in the winter. Reducing your filtration by 50 percent may save you more than $20 per month. Be sure to filter before 11 A.M. and/or after 5 P.M.

6. *Keep filter, skimmer, and strainer basket clean.* When your pump motor doesn't work as hard, it costs less to operate.

7. *Don't overclean.* Automatic pool-sweeping devices can usually get the job done in three to four hours a day in the summer and two to three hours a day during the off-season. But remember to set the cleaner to start 15 minutes before your filter. Again, try to operate the sweep outside the hours of 11 A.M. to 5 P.M.

Waterbed

Improperly controlled, waterbed energy costs could make you lose sleep. These tips will save you a lot of money.

1. *Don't unplug the bed during the day.* Getting the bed up to temperature every night uses more energy than operating the bed continuously with thermostat control.

2. *Make the bed every morning.* Controlled tests have shown that

beds with mattress pad sheets, cotton quilt, one blanket, and one-inch foam rubber mat between mattress and pad save about $15 a month over one covered by just sheets.

As you begin to put these various tips into practice, you will begin to see real savings on your monthly energy bills!

Saving Time and Money

A man who refuses to admit his mistakes can never be successful. But if he confesses and forsakes them, he gets another chance.

—Proverbs 28:13

*T*IME AND MONEY: We never seem to have enough of either of them, do we? Actually, we can control both time and money so that they work efficiently for us.

Here are some practical household tips that can help you save both time and money on a daily basis.

Saving Time

1. Plan a weekly menu and base your shopping list just on those menus. Then add to your list those staples which are getting low. Make sure your list is complete before you go shopping; it will save you time and gasoline.

2. Avoid trips to the market for single items.

3. Never shop for food when you're hungry; you may be tempted to deviate from your shopping list!

4. Plan your timetable for meal preparation so that your broccoli is not done ten minutes before the chicken and thereby loses color, texture, flavor, and nutritive value.

5. If you have such conveniences as a microwave oven or food processor, take advantage of them by incorporating them into your time schedule and menu for the week.

6. Organize your kitchen and save steps. Keep your most-used cookbooks and utensils in an area close at hand.

7. Save salad preparation time by washing and tearing salad greens once a week. Store them in an airtight container such as Tupperware.

8. Learn to do two things at the same time. When talking on the telephone you can: load the dishwasher, clean the refrigerator, cook a meal, bake a cake, mop the floor, or clean under the kitchen sink. I do recommend getting a long extension cord on your telephone!

9. Shell and chop your fresh pecans and walnuts while watching television. Then store them in the freezer or refrigerate them in airtight bags. When baking day arrives you'll be all set.

10. Convenience foods are worth their extra cost when time is short. A stock of frozen pastry shells, for example, will enable you to make a quiche or cream pie in very little time.

Saving Money

Here are some tips to keep in mind when planning your weekly menu.

1. Seasonal produce is usually your best buy. Green beans, in season, cost less per serving than canned beans and offer much more nutrition. Fresh produce also has better flavor and fewer additives.

2. High-ticket items are placed at eye level at most grocery stores. Check the top and bottom shelves for similar items with lower pricetags.

3. Avoid impulse buying, if it's not on your list, don't buy it.

4. Check your local newspaper ads for sales, especially in the meat section.

5. When things are on sale, consider buying them in larger quantities. For example, a dozen cans of tuna can be stored indefinitely.

6. Stay within your budget. Take a small notepad or calculator to the store so that you can keep a running total.

7. Take advantage of coupons, but only buy the product if it is already on your shopping list. Although this seems tedious, I know women who save $5.00 and more on their weekly grocery bill by using coupons.

8. Buy cheese in bricks. Slice or grate it at home to save the cost of handling and packaging.

9. Compare prices. For example, whole chicken breasts with ribs are about half the price of boned chicken breasts. If you want boned chicken, buy whole chicken breasts and parboil them for 10 to 12 minutes, and the meat will peel right off the bone.

10. Turn your unused bread crusts or not-quite-fresh bread and crackers into crumbs by using your blender. Use your crumbs in stuffing, casseroles, and meatloaf.

11. Save the oil from deep-frying. Strain it through cheesecloth and then refrigerate it.

12. Citrus fruit yields more juice when stored at room temperature.

13. Look into using special services and conveniences that don't cost extra money. For example, shopping from catalogs is one way to streamline your schedule and save time.

By putting even half of these ideas into action, you'll be surprised at how much time and money you'll save!

29

Great Fund-Raising Ideas

Happiness comes to those who are
fair to others and are always just
and good.

—Psalm 106:3

*M*ANY OF US are members of churches,
clubs, fraternities, or sororities that are
looking for ways to raise funds. About the time we realize there is a
need to raise funds, we scratch our heads to think of creative ways to
supplement our budget. Our minds go blank! Some of these ideas
from our readers can help you.

• **Service, Time, and Talent Auction.** In this auction you don't
sell material possessions but pledges for service, time, and talent.
Items you might include: baby-sitting, a resort area condominium,
home-baked cookies once a month for a year, car service to and from
the airport for a future plane trip. Each donation is the generous
giving of self.

• **Cleanup Crew.** A great high school or teenage project is to take
the place of professional street cleaners when you need to clean the
streets of the fall leaves. Charge the neighbors or business tenants a
fair wage scale. It doesn't take many students to earn a substantial
amount of money for their special project.

• **Hill of Beans.** Here's a fund-raiser that's literally a hill of beans—kidneys, pintos, lentils, split peas, garbanzos, limas, and more. Members of your club can donate these beans. Combine them into a colorful, flavorful mix, which are then bagged in plastic baggies of two cups each and sold for $2.00 along with instructions for rinsing, soaking, and making soup. Tie a colorful ribbon at the top of your bag to provide colorful eye appeal.

• **Lip Sync.** Hold a lip-sync show. While a recording of a real singer plays, each child performs one or two songs, imitating the artist's style and mouthing the lyrics. Have rehearsals so the students can pool the songs, tapes, records, and lyrics. You can even make costumes with materials on hand and such finishing touches as feathers or jewelry. Sell tickets or take a freewill offering. This is a good source for added funds.

• **Krazy Kalendar.** For your special fund-raiser, make up a unique calendar where you can preprint for specific days of the month specified money to put away for this fund-raising idea. For example, during a typical week in July ask for 50 cents on Sunday "if you didn't go to church tonight," followed by "one cent for each year of your age above 21" on Monday, "ten cents if you have a patio or deck" on Tuesday, "25 cents if you turned on the air conditioner" on Wednesday, "five cents for each glass of water you drank" on Thursday, "one cent for each page of a book you read" on Friday, and "ten cents if you drank lemonade" on Saturday. Deposit the money in a jar and contribute jointly for your special fund-raiser.

• **House Numbers.** Raise extra money by painting street numbers on the curbs of your neighborhood streets. Be sure to clear the idea with your local police department. Call on the neighbors to presell the orders. Depending on the economic level of your neighborhood, a fair price would be in the $3.00 to $5.00 range. Stencil black numbers in white 6 x 10 inch rectangles on curbs, steps, and sidewalks. You might even have local merchants donate the paint. You will find that the police and fire departments are usually delighted with the easy-to-read addresses.

• **Tasting Bee.** If you are passing up the usual barbecues, fish fries, pancake breakfasts, etc. you might want to try something different to make money— a "May Tasting Bee." At theme tables decorated with flowers, flags, and costumed dolls representing various parts of the world, you can serve portions of a variety of American, European, Mexican, and Oriental foods. For a fixed price you can sample food from as many tables as you wish. The dessert table could be an extra cost if you wish. The only eating utensils needed should be teaspoons and toothpicks. You could also preprint the food recipes and sell them for a nominal cost.

• **20 Talents.** Give your group of 20 youngsters $1.00 each to purchase supplies for a craft or baking project. You can also pool your money for larger projects. You can even contribute a little extra money on your own if you like. You can also use materials found around the house. In three or four weeks you can bring the crafts or baked goods to a central area in which they can be sold. You can turn the original $20.00 into much more than this by selling or auctioning off cookies, cakes, holiday decorations, aprons, stuffed toys, baby quilts, or covered photograph albums.

• **Seesaw Marathon.** Schedule a seesaw contest within your group and seesaw from a Friday afternoon until Sunday afternoon. You can presell pledges from you neighbors, friends, and family based on the number of hours the students can keep going. The students can teeter-totter in three-hour shifts.

Use your own creative imagination in creating your fund-raising projects. These efforts bring out the organizational ability of the various members and tend to bring the members closer together. Those who participate in these projects also become more familiar in the sponsoring group's purposes.

Fund-raising can be fun!

30

Organizing and Retrieving Records for Your Income Tax Report

> Better is a little with righteousness
> than vast revenues without justice.
>
> —*Proverbs 16:18* NKJV

*J*ENNY, where are the canceled checks for Dr. Merrihew?" Does this sound familiar around your home as you prepare for the annual April 15 deadline? Much unnecessary stress is caused in our households when we don't properly plan organizational details to help us as we prepare for our yearly IRS reports.

For many of us, we can complete the short form and claim the standard deductions and mail the forms off. However, for those who itemize our deductions, we have the responsibility to keep thorough records.

Beginning with 1987 and going through 1989 we found ourselves adapting to new tax laws (and it looks like the changes will continue). For those of you who have figured your own tax forms in the past, now might be the time to look into a professional tax-preparer.

Several years ago my husband, Bob, and I searched for a qualified tax professional who was a CPA, and we have been pleased with the additional refunds we have received because that person thoroughly understands the tax laws. With the coming changes, a professional preparer can more than save you the service charge to properly figure your new tax forms. Since his or her time usually costs by the number of schedules to prepare and the length of time it takes, you will save many dollars by having your records complete when you meet for your appointment. A little planning will save you a lot in the end.

Many of us have different styles of organization. Sally Sanguine can't be bothered each month to keep accurate records, so she tosses all her receipts, pay stubs, bank statements, canceled checks, and receipts (cash and charge) into a drawer or shoe box until tax time. At the end of the year she dumps all her materials on a tabletop or the floor and begins to sort. This type of record-keeping takes four to six hours to process. If you have several schedules with a small business, rental property, stock transactions, etc. you might spend up to three or four days to complete the forms.

If this is your style (and it can work) you can simplify the task by filing the receipts in an accordion file folder or large 9 x 12 envelopes. Total and staple each category and write the total at the top sheet of the category. Then record your totals on a worksheet. At this point you are ready to complete your own tax forms, or you can meet with your tax-preparer. Treat yourself to a bowl of ice cream or popcorn. In order to function under this method you have to have the right mindset. You are making a trade-off of small increments of time each month for a larger block of time once a year.

Many of us function better by staying on top of our record-keeping in smaller blocks of time. Some people prefer daily, some weekly, and some monthly. Whatever your desire, you need some basic tools to start your record-keeping.

- Regular or legal-size manila file folders (multicolored make the task cheerier and brightens up the task).
- A metal file cabinet (two-drawer minimum).
- Your local stationery store carries standard-size boxes to house such yearly records.
- Accordion-type file folder.
- Regular or legal-size envelopes.
- Wide felt pen for labeling your headings.
- Highlighter pen for marking receipt totals (for ease in identification when summarizing).

There are several ways to categorize your records. Select one that best fits your style of organization. Make a list of all items that will be income items and all expenses that are tax-deductible.

Income

- Salary—head of household
- Salary—spouse
  These records must include total wages, federal tax withheld, FICA, and state and local taxes. This information should appear on your W-2 form.
- Income listed on a 1099 form should be included.
- Alimony received (excluding child support)
- Interest and dividend income
- Income from sale of property, stocks, mutual funds, etc. Consult your tax-preparer for short-term or capital-gains implication.
- Royalties, commissions, fees
- Bonuses and prizes
- Tips and gratuities
- Annuities and pension income
- Lump-sum distribution from retirement plans
- Unemployment compensation. Note this even though it may not be taxable.
- Social Security benefits
- Veteran's benefits
- Workman's Compensation
- Other income

Expenses and Deductions

- Adoption expenses
- Alimony paid
- Casualty losses. Include auto accidents, fire, theft, storms, property damage, etc. List the loss, the value, and insurance payment, if any.
- Charitable work. Document expenses such as transportation, special clothing, and food and lodging if out of town.
- Childcare and dependent-care expenses
- Contributions, including tithes and offerings. List the name of the organization and the amount. Keep a receipt or canceled check.
- Doctors and dentists. This includes the amount of the bill as well as transportation or mileage on all trips.
- Finance charges on contracts
- Interest paid on all loans or mortgages
- Investment expenses. Include supplies, publications, transportation, cost of safe deposit box.

- Job-related expenses. This could include auto, special shoes, tools, uniforms, union dues, education expenses, professional dues and journals, safety equipment, transportation to a second job, job-seeking expenses, and employment agency fees.
- Medical insurance (premiums)
- Medication and drugs. Include prescriptions, vitamins/diet supplements if prescribed, and some over-the-counter drugs.
- Other medical expenses. Include eye exams, eyeglasses, ambulance, artificial limbs, hearing aids, lab tests, X-rays, acupuncture, chiropractors, nursing care, etc.
- Service charges and carrying charges on credit cards, cash reserves, etc.
- Tax (income, sales, state, and estimated taxes paid during the year)
- Tax-preparation costs

Some of these expense deductions will change in future years under new tax laws. It is always a good idea to check with the IRS literature for the next year. Call 1 (800) 829-1040 for IRS questions.

Once you have determined which of the income and expense items relate to your family's organizational needs, you can:

- Label a file folder for each income or deductible topic. When you have an item to file away, you can use the front of the envelope as a journal for writing down the date, to whom, and the amount of the entry. At the end of the year you just total the items listed on the front of the envelope and you have the totals for that entry. Inside your envelope you have all the receipts and stubs to back up your final total.
- Store these envelopes in your metal file folder, your cardboard box that you purchased from the local stationery store, or your accordion file. The method you use will be determined by how complicated your tax returns will be.

I have found that household receipts can be organized in a very simple way by using a regular legal-size folder. Just open it flat and glue onto each side of the folder three legal-size white envelopes. Label each envelope for the receipts:

A. utilities	D. medical
B. donations	E. insurance
C. credit cards	F. food

Set up one of these file folders for each month of the year, using your wide felt pen to label one folder for each month of the year. Each month as you pay bills, just slip the receipts into the proper envelope and file away. One added step speeds up the year-end process: Total the receipts in each envelope each month and write the total of the contents on the front of each of the individual envelopes. When tax time comes you will have all you need and can retrieve it quickly.

The IRS requires that you keep your records for a minimum of six years for most records. However, you will need to keep real estate and investment records longer if you will need to verify purchase prices in the future. Take particular care when relocating your residence. You do not want to lose these records in transit; in case of an audit you will find the reconstruction of your records to be very time-consuming and in some cases quite costly.

With a little thought and preparation you can have a system that is easy and that reduces stress and tension when your husband asks you to find where Dr. Merrihew's canceled checks are. He too will be able to retrieve this information quickly. Review together if you are married, because none of us knows when an emergency might occur for the other partner. Let's not keep our records a mystery!

Seven Steps to Financial Cleanup at Tax Time

A prudent man foresees the
difficulties ahead and
prepares for them.
—*Proverbs 22:3*

*Y*OU CAN DO a great financial clean-up yourself by breaking the job down into logical steps. Throwing everything out and making a clean start isn't the answer. Discarding salary stubs, last year's tax return, or current receipts for medical or business expenses will only bring you problems further down the road.

One of the biggest mistakes people make is not retaining records. Throwing away records that later turn out to be important cause people a lot of unnecessary work and worry. Well-kept financial records will pay off during emergencies. Should an accident occur, a friend or family member can quickly locate your insurance policy and the papers needed for vital information.

Here are seven steps to help have "More Hours in Your Day" during tax-return time.

1. *Know what to keep.* Keep permanent, lifetime records. These would include personal documents required for credit, job-qualification papers, Social Security and government program papers, birth and marriage certificates, Social Security number

119

cards, property records, college credits, diplomas, and licenses. Also keep *transitory records*. These pertain to your current circumstances: employee benefits, receipts for major purchases (auto, stock, jewelry, art), tax returns, insurance policies, credit union information, and canceled checks relating directly to home improvements.

The IRS has the right to audit within six years. Let this be a measure of how long you keep receipts, etc.

2. Set up your personal system according to your natural organization. If you are disorganized, your system should be simple. Keep it uncomplicated.

The less time you have, the simpler your system should be. If you like working with numbers and are good in math, your system can be more complex.

The simplest way to begin is to obtain two folders for receipts. Use the first folder for probable deductions and the second folder for questionable deductions. At tax time match deductible items or set up a system with folders for various deductions: medical, business, taxes, home, etc. When you pay a bill or get a receipt, simply drop it in the proper folder.

3. Set aside a spot for your records. Obtain a safe deposit box for permanent documents plus a fireproof and waterproof file cabinet for home use.

4. Let someone know where your records are kept. Make a list of the location of your insurance policies and give it to a family member, a friend, or even your pastor.

5. Get professional advice when you need it. Expert advice can go a long way and in the long run save you time and money. Accountants are a great source of information and many times save much more than their cost. Financial planners are helpful if your past history has been a financial disaster, and they can benefit you by helping you avoid future mistakes.

6. Change your system depending upon your season of life, such as marriage, self-employment, or vocational change. What works now may not work five years from now. What worked last year may need some revisions this year.

7. Record-keeping requires time set aside. You must discipline yourself to set aside a time each month on a consistent basis to go over your financial records so you won't be overwhelmed in April when you have to file your tax return. Some people update weekly when paying bills or when reconciling checking accounts.

Great record-keeping gives mental benefits as well as "More Hours" to do things you enjoy doing.

God will honor and bless you as you keep order in your financial life.

Holidays

32

Holiday Safety Survival Checklist

Suddenly there appeared with the
angel a multitude of the heavenly
host, praising God and saying,
"Glory to God in the highest, and
on earth peace among men with
whom He is pleased."
—Luke 2:13,14

*T*HE HOLIDAYS are supposed to be fun, relaxing, spiritual, and festive.

This Christmas safety checklist will help you and your family have a safe and merry Christmas! Taking these simple safety precautions throughout the season will prevent mishaps and help you enjoy the holidays even more.

Tips:

- Don't overload electrical circuits.
- Use only the replacement bulbs and fuses recommended by the manufacturer.
- Replace broken or burned-out bulbs in old strings of lights, unplugging them before you do.
- Keep strings of lights unplugged when hanging them on the tree.
- Use clips specially made for hanging lights on the house. Misdirected nails and staples can damage or expose wires.
- Don't use indoor lights outside.

- Do not use lights with worn or frayed cords, exposed wires, broken or cracked sockets, or loose connections.
- Check all electrical lights, cords, and connections before you decorate.
- Use a heavy-duty extension cord with a ground, and never string more than three standard-size sets of lights per single extension cord.
- Follow the directions and heed the cautions on the packaging of any lighting products you purchase.
- Safety experts recommend using electrical fixtures that carry the approval label of Underwriters Laboratory (UL).
- The Red Cross warns that many holiday plants are poisonous and can cause serious illness. Holly, mistletoe, yew, and Jerusalem cherry plants should never be chewed or swallowed.
- All parts of the poinsettia also are dangerous, they contain toxins that can irritate the mouth, throat, stomach and eyes. If swallowed, seek prompt medical attention. Keep all holiday plants out of the reach of children.
- To avoid electrical shock, do not use electrical decorations on trees with metallic needles, leaves, or branches. Use color spotlights above or beside a metallic tree.
- Burning evergreens in a fireplace is dangerous; flames can flare out and send sparks flying about the room. Give your tree to the garbage collector.
- Equip your home with a UL-listed, ABC-rated fire extinguisher and smoke or heat detectors. They make good stocking stuffers.
- Be careful with fire salts, which produce colored flames on wood fires. They cause severe stomach disorders if swallowed. Keep them away from children.
- Make sure your tree is fresh when you buy it. As the needles turn brown and begin to break off easily, the tree becomes a greater fire risk. Keep the tree-base holder filled with water at all times. Place the tree in a location away from the fireplace, radiator, and other heat sources. Be sure it is out of your home traffic pattern and doesn't block a doorway.
- Never use lighted candles on a tree or near evergreens or draperies.
- Never use aluminum foil or differently-rated fuses to replace burned-out electric fuses.
- If you buy an artificial tree, make sure it has been UL-tested for flammability.
- Buy toys for infants and toddlers that are too large to fit into their mouths. Be sure the eyes on dolls and the buttons on stuffed animals are secure.

- Buy toys appropriate for a child's age and development.
- Be sure electrical toys are tested for safety. Look for the UL mark.
- Throw away gift wrappings immediately. Don't burn them in the fireplace. They can ignite suddenly and cause a flash fire.
- Always turn off tree lights before leaving home or going to bed.
- When removing your tree lights, wind them around the tube from a roll of paper towels. Start collecting tubes now. It will make for fast, easy storage and easy tree trimming next year.
- Store ornaments in apple-type boxes; layer newspaper or tissue paper between ornaments to prevent breakage.
- Store extension cords in toilet paper tubes and keep them with your tree lights so you'll have them when needed next year.
- Don't forget wrapping paper, cards, and Christmas ribbons go on sale the week after Christmas at 50 to 70 percent off, so stock up for next year and save money.

Blessings for a happy holiday and a safe New Year!

33

Fall Harvest Pumpkin Times

If we are living in the light of
God's presence, just as Christ does,
then we have wonderful fellowship
and joy with each other.

—1 John 1:7

*S*UMMER IS about over and as the nip hits
the air and the leaves begin to turn burnt
red and orange, it's time to hang the corn on your door and put Mr.
Pumpkin in place for the fall season.

Even though we live in the city our home is country. By mid-
September our corn season is about over and the stalks from our
summer garden are tied and placed around the front door of the
house. One package of pumpkin seeds planted last May gave us an
overabundant supply of fresh, bright orange pumpkins. We not only
had enough for our home but enough to supply the neighborhood. We
then made Mr. Scarecrow out of an old pair of Bob's blue jeans and a
plaid shirt stuffed with newspapers . . . so easy. A pair of garden
gloves for his hands and a pumpkin for his head—we painted the face
and placed a straw hat to top it off! All the children loved our harvest
scene and it was enjoyed until late November.

Harvest ideas are a treat to create. Take your pick of these ideas
and establish your own family traditions.

1. If you are proud of your carved harvest pumpkins and want to

keep them in firm shape indefinitely, simply spray their insides and outsides with an antiseptic, repeating periodically as necessary. The antiseptic destroys the bacteria that normally grow and soften the pumpkins.

2. Don't throw out the pumpkin seeds when you are through carving. Salt the seeds and dry them in the oven on a cookie sheet for a tasty, nutritious snack the whole family will love.

3. A hollowed pumpkin makes a creative punch bowl for apple cider. It can also be used for a harvest soup tureen. There are recipes for pumpkin soup and spiced tea in my book *The Complete Holiday Organizer* (Harvest House).

4. Many local churches, parks, recreation departments, and community centers provide fun harvest activities, a phone call can give you the schedule of events.

5. Take your family to a local pumpkin patch. There are many commercial pumpkin fields in various areas across the country. Often you can harvest your own pumpkin right from the grower's field. If not, consider planting your own patch next year like we did.

No thumping is necessary to determine pumpkin ripeness: Once it is orange a pumpkin is ready to use. It will last for months if not cut or broken or cracked. It's best not to lift pumpkins by the stem as they often break off.

Take home several for Halloween carving and Thanksgiving pumpkin pies.

This is a fun outing particularly for city families. Many of these patches will have cornstalks, gourds, and Indian corn, which make excellent materials for harvest decoration both at the front door and dining room table. Ask the farmer if you could bring a picnic lunch and share a family time in the midst of the vines.

6. Carving faces on the pumpkins is a fun experience for the family. Children love to be involved in making funny faces, but care needs to be taken when carving. A sharp knife used by either a child who is too young or by a child who hasn't been shown the proper use of a knife can ruin a good time. Colored paint-pens are a great option and can be purchased at craft and art supply stores.

7. Plan a neighborhood pumpkin carving or pumpkin painting party:

• Spread several layers of newspapers on the driveway, kitchen countertop, garage floor, or basement (depending on the weather).

• Carve or draw faces on the pumpkins, each person creating his or her own masterpiece. Children can use the paint pens or felt marking pens.

• Cut into the pumpkin and separate seeds from pulp. (See number 2 above on how to roast seeds.)

• After each pumpkin is carved, put a candle inside. In the bottom of the pumpkin carve a shallow hole so the candle will fit in an upright position. A little melted wax in the hole will also help secure the candle. A votive candle in a glass container works best if available.

• Display your pumpkin in the window, on the table, or on your front porch. Make sure there is no fire danger near the candle.

• After the carving session you might want to finish off the evening with hot apple cider, popcorn, and your roasted pumpkin seeds. Truly an evening to remember.

• For baby pumpkins use oranges. A fun project is to decorate with faces using, again, the marking pens. The decorated oranges can also be used as a nutritious snack and put into lunch sacks during the harvest season.

• Make pumpkin faces on a cheese sandwich. Cut the jack-o'-lantern face on one side of bread. Add cheese and second slice of bread. Serve plain or toasted under the broiler. A cleaner combination is dark rye bread with yellow cheese.

• Create these and other fun memories during this special harvest pumpkin time. Plan several harvest walks as a family and collect leaves, acorns, pods, and berries. These can all be placed around your pumpkins on the table for your harvest centerpiece.

The Busy Person's Thanksgiving Dinner

Let us not get tired of doing what is
right, for after a while we will reap
a harvest of blessing.
—*Galatians 6:9*

*T*ODAY'S BUSY WOMEN just don't have
the time to do what great grandma did.
She cooked for days until Thanksgiving arrived. Last Thanksgiving
I found myself in the middle of a busy holiday seminar schedule. The
thought of roasting a turkey, cleaning the house, and getting the
trimmings together for Thanksgiving dinner caused my stress level
to elevate to dangerous heights!

I stopped to take a deep breath and think long enough to come up
with a solution to my busyness. I decided to make our harvest dinner
a potluck. I made a few phone calls and quickly organized a simple
meal.

Here are some of the steps I took. Try them out this year for your
best-ever Thanksgiving.

Step 1

Develop your Thanksgiving dinner menu. Here is a sample menu:

Turkey, dressing, cranberry sauce: You will do this.
Vegetable: Auntie Syd
Potato or rice: Grandma Gertie
Rolls: Uncle Blair
Relish dish: Brad and Marie
Pumpkin pie: Craig and Jenny

Step 2

Phone your guests to invite them for a Busy Person's Thanksgiving Dinner. For your own reference, make a simple chart or list with their name and what item they will be bringing. (For example: Vegetable—Aunt Amy; Relish dish—Sister Sue.)

Ask them to please call an RSVP to you at least 10 days before Thanksgiving dinner. This way you'll still have time to adjust things if someone can't make it after all.

Step 3

Get your family involved. Assign the name cards to one child or to your husband to write a Scripture verse on the back or inside of each individual card. These verses should fit the Thanksgiving holiday; for example, Ephesians 5:20, "Always giving thanks for all things in the name of our Lord Jesus Christ" (NASB).

Use a 3 x 5 card folded in half, placing the name on the front and the Scripture inside. These will be read aloud by each person before your meal.

Step 4

Have another child make cards titled "I'm thankful for. . . ." These should be given to your guests when they first arrive at your home, so they have time to think about their response.

After dinner each guest will read their thankful card. This is a great way to focus on the positive things God provides for us. Or you could have a person interview each guest, asking the question, "What is the best thing that has happened to you this year (month, week, today)?" This exercise has given our family many great times of communication and often brought tears from each of us.

Step 5

Make out your grocery list for what you will need for the big day. As hostess you will be providing the turkey, dressing, and cranberry sauce.

Step 6

A few days before turkey day, make sure you have everything you will need for setting the table—including a centerpiece. Keep it simple by using a pumpkin surrounded by fresh fruit or three candles in autumn colors with designed holders. (Votive candles floating in a glass or bowl of water also work well as a centerpiece.) To save time, try to use something you already have on hand.

Step 7

Prepare your thawed turkey for roasting in the late afternoon on the day before Thanksgiving.

I recommend my "Perfect Every Time Turkey Recipe." I have found it to be a lifesaver for the busy woman. I've adapted the recipe from Adelle Davis' book *Let's Cook It Right* (New American Library, 1947). I've used this recipe for 32 years and never had it fail me yet!

Recipe

Preheat oven to 350 degrees.

Wash turkey well and remove the neck and giblets. Dry turkey with paper towels, salt the cavity, and stuff with dressing of your choice. Rub the outside of the turkey with pure olive oil. Stick a meat thermometer into the turkey.

Place the turkey breast-down in the roasting pan on a rack (this way the breast bastes itself, keeping the meat moist). Roast the turkey one hour at 350 degrees to destroy bacteria on the surface. Then adjust the heat to 180 or 200 degrees for any size turkey. The turkey can roast in the oven on this low temperature 15 to 30 hours before you eat it. A good rule for timing is to allow about one hour per pound of meat.

For example, a 20-pound turkey that takes 15 minutes per pound to roast would take five hours by the conventional, fast-cooking method. The slow method is one hour per pound, so it would take 20 hours to roast.

I usually begin roasting a 22-pound turkey at 5 P.M. Thanksgiving Eve. I put the turkey in the oven and leave it uncovered until it's done the next day between 1 P.M. and 3 P.M.

Although the amount of cooking time seems startling at first, the meat turns out amazingly delicious, juicy, and tender. It slices beautifully, barely shrinks in size, and vitamins and proteins are not harmed because of the low cooking temperature.

Once the turkey is done, it will not overcook. You can leave it in an additional three to six hours, and it will still not dry out. It browns perfectly and you'll get wonderful drippings for gravy.

Thanksgiving Countdown

Happy is the generous man, the one
who feeds the poor.
—*Proverbs 22:9*

𝒯HE FIRST national Thanksgiving proclamation was issued by George Washington in 1789. In 1863 President Abraham Lincoln made a Thanksgiving Day proclamation to establish this as a national holiday of thanksgiving to be observed on the last Thursday in November. In 1941 Congress changed the day to the fourth Thursday in November, which is where it has stayed.

For the last 100 years in America, we have been developing meaningful traditions to make this one of the most memorable of all holidays.

Thanksgiving is warm hearts, good food, family, and *lots* of conversation.

It is said that 60 percent of our stress is caused by disorganization. If Thanksgiving brings stress to your mind, it could very well be because of disorganization. So let's relieve that stress. Step by step let's count down the things we can do to make this holiday season stress-less. This will give us time and energy to build memories with our families and friends.

First Week in November

Activity   *Done (X)*
- Polish silver ....
- Plan guest list ....
- Send invitations ....
(or a cheery phone invitation is always welcome)

Second Week in November

Activity   *Done (X)*
- Plan menu ....
- Begin marketing list ....
- Plan table setting..............................
- Plan centerpiece ....
- List what you may need to borrow and
reserve those items ....

Third Week in November

Activity   *Done (X)*
- Make name place cards. As a family you can each find verses with a thankful theme. Take a 3 x 5 card, fold it in half and stand it up on the table. On the front write the name of the person who will sit at that place and inside write the thankful verse of Scripture. When everyone is seated on Thanksgiving Day, each person reads his verse. This can serve as the blessing ....
- Have prepared 3 x 5 cards and a pen at each person's seat and have the person write something for which they are thankful. These can be read during or before or after the meal ....
- Begin to buy some of the staples at the market you will need for that Thanksgiving feast. It will help the budget that last week. Canned cranberry sauce, dressing mix, canned green beans, etc. ....
- Plan your baking day ....

Fourth Week in November

By now I'm really excited about all the things that I've done and so thankful I've already accomplished so much toward our special day.

Activity   *Done (X)*
- Plan and organize serving dishes . . . .
- Make out a 3 x 5 card for each dish and list on the card what will go into the empty dish. This way you don't have to remember at the last minute what goes where. It also makes it easy for guests to help with the final preparations . . . .
- Check marketing list to be sure you've got on it just what you'll need for each recipe . . . .
- The day before Thanksgiving set the table and set centerpiece on the table . . . .
- Place Scripture name cards at each place. . . . .
- Put serving silverware on the table to be put into each serving dish . . . .
- Bake pies . . . .
- Check menu and recipes one more time. . . . .

Perhaps you are not preparing a Thanksgiving dinner yourself, but may be taking a dish to someone's home. Your organization will be simpler but should also be planned ahead of time. Ingredients purchased and time set aside for preparation and cooking can be planned ahead as well. Even if you aren't taking food, a hostess gift is always nice: a bouquet of flowers, small plant, stationery, jar of jam, crackers and cheese, etc. Remember, even if you gave a verbal thank-you it is always good manners to follow up with a written note.

As you gather around the Thanksgiving table, holding hands can make this a special family and friendship time. "We give thanks to God, the Father of our Lord Jesus Christ" (Colossians 1:3). Have a beautiful turkey day filled with love and thanksgiving to God—and don't forget to serve the cranberry sauce and garnish the platter with parsley.

Week After Thanksgiving

Activity   *Done (X)*
- Put away fall decorations . . . . ,
- Start thinking toward Christmas . . . .

Activity   *Done (X)*
- Week 1 . . . . ,
- Week 2 . . . .
- Week 3 . . . .
- Week of . . . .
- Week after . . . .

Christmas Countdown

*Unto us a Child is born; unto us a
Son is given. . . . His royal titles:
"Wonderful," "Counselor," "The
Mighty God."*
—Isaiah 9:6

*B*EING BUSY homemakers, with many women also working outside the home, puts added pressure on us as the holiday season arrives. However, if we can plan ahead and organize our holidays, we will find it a joy instead of feeling, "Oh no, not Christmas again!" Proverbs 16:3 says that we are to commit our works to the Lord, and our *plans* will be established.

As we begin this Holiday Countdown let's first give these next weeks to our Lord, remembering to give thanks for *all* things and trusting Him to help us establish our holiday plans and priorities.

Take time to share the true meaning of the holidays with your friends and family.

December Countdown

Christmas is a loving and giving time. Take time to love: Send a card to a shut-in; sing a song at a convalescent home; smile a greeting as you shop.

- Address Christmas cards and mail early in the month.

- Make Christmas gift list.
- Plan baking days for the month. Include at least one baking day for the children to help with cookies and candies.
- Plan a craft day for the family to make tree ornaments. Felt, noodles, ice cream sticks, pine cones, and thread spools can all be used to create ornaments. String popcorn and cranberries for the tree. Keep in mind the family unit working together.
- Shop early.
- Wrap gifts early.
- Keep in mind giving handmade and homemade items such as jams, breads, pot holders, and tree ornaments as gifts.
- Attend a Christmas boutique. There you will be able to purchase beautiful handmade items at reasonable prices.
- Decorate your home early in the month so you can enjoy the holiday as long as possible.
- Decorate your front door with a wreath made of pine branches, pine cones, and ribbon, and incorporate a small nativity scene keeping Christ in Christmas. Your front door will give a warm welcome to all who enter your loving home, apartment, mobile home, condominium, or whatever place you call home.

Suggested Stocking Stuffers

- Small stuffed teddy bears
- Paint sets and brushes
- Colored pens or pencils
- Art paper for projects
- Puzzles, books, small Bible
- Marbles, jacks
- Subscription to magazine
- Clothing items such as socks, tights, hosiery, belts, barrettes, headbands, or other hair items
- Music tapes
- Photos (framed)
- Posters
- Theater tickets for a special play, amusement park tickets (Disneyland, etc.)
- Balloons with a dollar bill tucked inside
- Nuts and fruits
- Toothbrush, shampoo, curling iron, hand lotion, perfume or cologne
- Kitchen items for mom
- Small garden tools and packaged seeds for dad

- Any hobby items
- Barbecue tools, picnic accessories
- Tupperware
- Flashlight
- Measuring tape
- Apron, kitchen towels
- Golf balls
- Tennis balls
- Etc. etc. etc.... This should get you started with suggested ideas!
- Plan a family "Happy Birthday Jesus" party:
    Bake a cake with candles.
    Read the Christmas story.
    Share memorable Christmases.
    Have a family communion.
    Sing "Happy Birthday" to Jesus.
- Make a Christmas Love Basket filled with food items, toys, clothing, and needed items for a needy family in your church or community. Sharing our Lord's love with others is what Christmas is all about.

37

Stressless Christmas

Not by might, nor by power, but by
my Spirit, says the Lord
Almighty—you will succeed
because of my Spirit.

—*Zechariah 4:6*

HOW FUN and relaxed you will be when you have stacked up creative gifts made by you and ready to give throughout this holiday season.

From the time I was a little girl, my mother taught me how to make fun, inexpensive gifts. Here are a few of those ideas to help you get gift-organized for Christmas.

- Give your favorite recipe written on a cute card and include two or three of the ingredients. Example: Chocolate chip oatmeal cookie recipe—include one package chocolate chips, one package nuts and several cups oatmeal in a zip-lock bag.
- Package in a zip-lock bag five to seven different kinds of dry beans and include your favorite bean soup recipe.
- Take baby food jars and apply cute stickers to the front. Three of these make a great gift for storing cotton balls, bath salts, Q-Tips, etc.
- Paint "Honey Pot" on the front of a jar and fill with honey. Tie a cute ribbon around the lid with a bow.

- Make Christmas ornaments out of different kinds of noodles, using Elmer's white glue.
- Cover shoeboxes with wrapping paper, wallpaper, contact paper, etc., and use as a gift box. Fill with stationery items—glue stick, small scissors, paper clips, marking pens, memo pad, and thank-you notes. Any mom, dad, grandparent, or teacher would love such a gift.
- How about covering a box with road maps and filling the box with more road maps, a first-aid kit, a teaching tape or your favorite music tape, jumper cables, flares, or any kind of item associated with travel and/or the car?
- Baskets make great gifts filled with items:

>Bath—soaps, shower cap, bubble bath, bath oil, washcloth

>Reading—book for each family member, bookmarks

>Kitchen—wooden spoons, measuring cups, can opener, etc.

>Toys—games, books, teddy bear, dolls, truck, puzzles, etc.

>Grandma—bib to use for grandbabies, toy, rattle, book of short stories, baby items, etc.

>Gardening—seeds, garden tools, gloves, pruners/clippers, hand shovel, fertilizer, potted plants

>Sewing—measuring tape, scissors, pins, jar of buttons, elastic lace, ribbon, tape, etc.

>Laundry—bleach, laundry powder or liquid, fabric softener, spray spot remover, small spot brush

>For men—car wax, chamois, Armor-all, trash bags, litter bag for car

Food items always make great gifts. Use resources that are in your area and available to you. Every year we receive a bag of raw peanuts. Oh, how we love and enjoy them for several months! Here are more food ideas:

- Popcorn
- Breads—banana, zucchini
- Nuts—almonds, walnuts
- Carmel corn
- Pure natural maple syrup
- Fruits—We have several orange trees on our property, so I fill a box or basket with oranges and send them to my uncle. He especially loves this gift and looks forward to it.

    Avocados

    Dried fruits

- Basket of natural foods such as granola mix, raisins, three-to-seven-grain cereal mix
- Bread starters

Many of these gift ideas can be prepared far ahead of time so that you will be able to relax and enjoy the holidays. Organization of gifts is one of the keys to a stressless Christmas. So plan and prepare ahead for a pleasant, organized holiday.

38

Holiday Hints
for You
and the Children

This is the day which the Lord hath
made; we will rejoice and be glad
in it.

—*Psalm 118:24* NKJV

*H*OLIDAY TIMES can be a fun time for children. It can also be a very hectic time for parents. What with presents, entertaining, cooking, and shopping . . . the children get so-o-o excited and seem to have more energy than at any other time of the year. This can be a season of learning for those energetic little ones as we channel that energy into helping us relieve the stress of the holiday "frenzies." Here are some Holiday Helps to bless you and the children.

Plan one or two baking days when the children help with holiday breads, cookies, or pies. Christ-centered cookie cutters such as stars, angels, crosses, and even Christmas trees are available. As you cut the cookies discuss with the little ones the Christmas story from the star to the wise men to the gifts the wise men brought. You can relate that one of the reasons we give gifts to others is to give our love to others as did the wise men gone to the Christ child. The Christmas and lights signify the shining stars and a place to put the gifts. As they decorate the cookies you can sing Christmas carols or play a holiday musical tape.

The cookies can be frozen for later use. A plate of cookies given to friends or neighbors can teach the children to give of their talents and the fruits of their labor. Plus what an outreach to those who receive Christ-centered cookies.

Depending upon the ages of the children they can help wrap presents. Comic strip sections from newspapers make good wrapping paper, or use white paper or tissue paper the children can rubber-stamp. Again, find a Christ-centered stamp with a manger scene or perhaps stars. Glue on candy kisses, candy canes, M & M's. Get creative—anything goes. If the gift is a cookbook or kitchen item, wrap it in a tea towel. If it's an educational book, use roadmaps as the paper. If it's handsewn, a measuring tape makes a cute bow. Get out lace pieces and rickrack to glue on and decorate the top. The children can design a lace collar for mom's gift, and for dad, a tie or bow tie. The children will be excited and invent all sorts of unusual gift wraps.

Make your own gift tags out of wrapping paper pieces or construction paper in red, green, or white; rubber-stamped to match the papers. You can also use wooden spoon ornaments, paper dolls, cookie cutters, key chains, shells, bookmarks, etc. Paint pens (which can be bought at craft or art supply stores) will write on almost anything and the color and print won't come off.

Capitalize if possible, on the hobby or vocation of the person whose gift you are wrapping. For the golfer, use golf tees tied onto the bow. For an artist, a new paint brush. For the mechanic, a new tool; the gardener, a new pair of gloves or seeds. For the craft lady or knitter, knitting needles or embroidery thread tied onto the bow.

Children will love this gift idea: Roll up a dollar bill and insert it into a balloon. Mail it along with a card and instructions to blow up the balloon and then pop it. Out comes the bill!

When planning your holiday party, buffet, open house, or family dinner, let the older children extend themselves by helping out with the little ones to give you extra time to shop and prepare. They can then have the privilege of taking part in greeting the guests, taking their coats, being polite, and using manners with a smile. They should also remember to say thank you and please. They can pass out hors d'oeuvres, pour water, coffee, tea, clear off tables, serve dessert, and blow out the candles. Cleanup help can also be part of learning. Throw some coins into the bottom of the kitchen sink beneath the sudsy water as a reward. One hundred pennies, four to eight quarters, 20 nickels, etc. On their pillow pin a big thank-you note saying, "Good job, well done!"

If you don't have children, borrow some just to help teach them manners and proper ways of entertaining.

A great gift that children can make is a personalized pillow or pillowcase. They can use paint pens in assorted colors or nontoxic acrylic paints to list a friend's important personal dates and memory places or perhaps his or her favorite Bible verse on the pillow. Grandparents' names can be put along with the children's handprints. Aprons also make great personalized gifts with the grandchildren's names printed on and/or their handprints. This is also a nice idea for teachers at school or Sunday school.

Homemade Christmas cards that children have cut out or colored are always appreciated. Last year's cards can be cut up and glued onto construction paper. Children can use stencils, rubber stamps, or their own creative designs. These can also be made into placemats. I've found that heavy-duty plastic, oval-shaped placemats (on sale) in a variety of colors work well. Or make the placemats out of heavy poster board and cover with clear plastic contact paper.

Let your and the children's creative juices flow as you guide them into helping you relieve some of the stress the holiday brings.

They will receive the blessings and you will be blessed as you watch their talents develop.

Organizing Holiday Meals

> The more lowly your service to others, the greater you are. To be the greatest, be a servant.
> —*Matthew 23:11*

*T*HE CRISP DAYS of late autumn bring on memories of holiday happenings, roast turkey, cranberry sauce, hot apple cider, family gatherings—and lest you forget, a lot of hard work. But with a bit of organization, holiday planning can be more stress-free and a lot of fun.

I've prepared a Hospitality Sheet for you on page 147 (Figure 4) that can be clipped out or easily reproduced for your convenience.

To show you how the chart works, here are a few ideas about how to fill it in.

One Week Before
- Prepare your menu.
- Make your shopping list.

Three Days Before
- Polish silver.
- Clean house as needed.

One Day Before
- Shop for groceries.
- Clean and prepare vegetables, grate cheese, and chop nuts.

- Set table and also place centerpiece, candles, and other decorations.

Day Of
- Cook your meal.
- Give yourself time to relax and dress before the guests arrive.

Last Minute
- Check your menu to see that you haven't forgotten anything such as the cranberry sauce or pickles.
- Enjoy your time with family and friends.

HOSPITALITY SHEET

Date _____   Place _____
Time _____   Number of Guests _____
Event _____   Theme _____

Menu	Recipe Preparation Time	Things To Do	✓
Hors D'Oeuvres/Appetizer		One Week Before	
Entree		Three Days Before	
Side Dishes		One Day Before	
Salad		Day of	
Dessert			
Drinks		Last Minute	

Guest List	RSVP		★ Notes ★	Supplies
	Yes	No		
				Tables/Chairs
				Dishes
				Silver
				Glasses

Figure 4

40

Holiday Kitchen Hints

The Lord himself will choose the
sign—a child shall be born to a
virgin! And she shall call him
Immanuel (meaning, "God is
with us").
—*Isaiah 7:14*

*T*HE HOLIDAY SEASON is a great time to renew old acquaintances, reconcile broken relationships, and reinforce existing friendships. It's a time for growing—growing through giving, through sharing, through serving. But most of all, it's a time to give thanks to a loving Father for all the little things we take for granted.

Hints

- If bread or cake browns too quickly before it is thoroughly baked, place a pan of warm water on the rack above it in the oven.
- To prevent icing from running off cake, dust a little cornstarch over the cake before icing.
- To add a new taste to oatmeal cookies, add a small amount of grated orange peel to the next batch.
- If you cover dried fruit or nuts with flour before adding them to the cake batter, they will not sink to the bottom during baking.
- The yolk of an egg will keep for several days if it is covered with cold water and placed in the refrigerator in a covered dish.

- Either parboil sausages or roll them in flour before frying to prevent them from bursting.
- If you have used too much salt while cooking, add a raw potato. This will absorb much of the salt.
- Tie herbs and spices in a piece of wet muslin or cheesecloth before adding them to soup or stew so that they may be easily removed when finished.
- Save the rinds of the oranges you squeezed for breakfast. Pile mounds of mashed sweet potatoes on them, then brown them in the oven.
- To keep old potatoes from darkening when they are boiling, add a small amount of milk to the cooking water.
- Pancakes will remain hot longer if the bottle of syrup which is to be served with them is first heated in hot water.
- Adding a pinch of salt in the basket will relieve some of the acid taste in perked coffee. For clear coffee, put egg shells in after perking. And remember, always start with cold water.
- Adding about 1½ teaspoonfuls of lemon juice to a cup of rice while cooking will keep the kernels separated.
- Baking apples or stuffed peppers in a well-greased muffin tin will help them keep their shape and look more attractive when served.
- Combining the juices from canned vegetables with soups will increase the quantity and flavor.
- Lumpy gravy? Pour it in your blender and in seconds it will be smooth.
- You'll shed fewer tears if you cut the root end of the onion off last.
- To eliminate spattering and sticking when pan-frying or sautéing, heat your pan before adding butter or oil. Not even eggs stick with this method.
- Muffins sticking to the tin pan? Place the hot pan on a wet towel. The muffins will slide right out.
- To tenderize tough meat or game: Make a marinade of equal parts cooking vinegar and heated bouillon. Marinate for two hours.
- To stew an old hen, soak it in vinegar for several hours before cooking. It will taste like a spring chicken!
- Instant white sauce: Blend together one cup soft butter and one cup flour. Spread in a 16-cube ice cube tray and chill. Store cubes in a plastic bag in the freezer. For medium thick sauce, drop one cube into one cup of milk and heat slowly, stirring as it thickens.

- Unmolding gelatin: Rinse the mold in cold water and coat with salad oil. Your molded salad will drop out easily and will have an appealing luster.
- Ridding the ham of the rind: Slit the rind lengthwise on the underside before placing ham in the roasting pan. As the ham bakes, the rind will pull away and can be removed easily without lifting ham.
- To keep olives or pimentos from spoiling, cover them with a brine solution of one teaspoonful of salt to one cup of water. Then float just enough salad oil over the top to form a layer about $1/8$-inch thick. Store them in the refrigerator.

Blessed holidays to all!

Surviving the Stress of Shopping

I will call upon the Lord, who is worthy to be praised; he will save me from all my enemies.

—2 Samuel 22:4

*M*ANY OF US who keep a busy schedule right through the holidays usually don't find time to shop for Christmas until after Thanksgiving.

With limited time to spend shopping, every minute must count—and organization is a key. Before you begin, plan your shopping strategy so that you can accomplish the majority of your shopping in one trip.

1. Review all the stores in the mall or downtown area you plan to shop in—such as jewelry, clothing, book, china, and hardware stores. (If you are really ambitious, write them all down.)

2. Decide before you go out what types of gifts you plan to purchase this year. For example, are you going to buy one big gift for each person or lots of little things? Each year I do things a bit differently.

3. Make your gift list based on the order of the shops within the particular shopping area you choose. Work your way around mentally, jotting down specific people and gift ideas.

4. Take advantage of wrapping services and/or gift boxes with ribbon and tissue. As much as possible, take home gifts that are ready to place under the tree.

5. Do two things at the same time. If, for example, you purchase clothing for more than one person at a store which offers gift wrapping, allow the clerk to finish the packages while you visit other shops. Circle back at the end of the day and collect your packages.

6. Think in categories. How many golfers, skiers, or tennis players are on your list? When buying for one, buy for the others. What about duplicate gifts? Can you give all your neighbors gourmet cheese in a can or spiced mustard in a jar? Why not?

7. Make use of your phone. Call your florist to make up a silk flower arrangement or a basket of soaps and hand creams. Or order a pretty holiday arrangement with a candle for the Christmas table centerpiece. Many times a florist will wrap and deliver your gift for you.

8. Give gift certificates to the hard-to-please people who have everything. Certificates for restaurants, ice-cream shops, and fast-food drive-ins (children love those) are always a hit.

9. Present a magazine subscription. Often magazines offer a gift subscription at a reduced price for the holidays. Include a current issue with your gift card.

10. Take a few breaks during your shopping to review your list and thoughts. Plan a coffee, tea, or lunch break. If you find yourself weighed down by too many packages, make a trip to lock them in the car.

11. Avoid retracing your steps or making second trips by not leaving a shopping area until you are sure you have accomplished all you wanted to do in that spot.

12. Assign shopping to a teenager or a friend who loves to shop.

13. Remember to keep your shopping simple. It is the love you put into each gift that will last rather than the gift alone. And more importantly, remember to make Christ the center of all your activities this Christmas.

Gift Wrap Organization for Gift-Giving

Today in the city of David there has
been born for you a Savior, who is
Christ the Lord.

—*Luke 2:11* NASB

*G*IFT GIVING really goes on all year. It is one of the major parts of our lives. The love of giving gifts goes on and on and on and on throughout the year.

Being creative with gift wrap is easy and can be inexpensive—like using newsprint to wrap dad's gift. The stock market, sports, travel, comic, or business section with Christmas ribbon is easy and original.

Perhaps you've saved those little pieces of wrapping paper thinking someday you would use them. Use them now! Simply tape together the pieces and make a patchwork gift wrap. Creative, original, and inexpensive.

Your plain paper or butcher paper can be used as a background for rubber-stamping, stickers, or vegetable prints. To make a potato print, cut a potato in half and carve a design into the potato; a heart, an angel, a Christmas tree, a star, a teddy bear, etc. Dip the potato into acrylic paint thinned with water, then stamp onto the brown paper. Thumbprint designs are unique and handprints are always fun. Collages can be made from old Christmas cards, pictures cut out of magazines, and newspapers. These can be taped or glued to plain paper and used as gift wrap.

Instead of bows on kitchen gifts, use a colored plastic or copper scouring pad, or colorful plastic measuring spoons. The name tag can be a wooden spoon with the "to" and "from" written on the handle with a felt pen.

Baby's gift can be wrapped in a clean disposable diaper or a cloth diaper. An ornament for baby's first Christmas can be tied to the package.

Gifts for sewing buffs can be wrapped in a remnant of fabric, tied with a tape measure, and pinned together (rather than using tape).

At the after-Christmas supplies sales you will find most gift wrap supplies marked down at least 50 percent. This is the time to buy—try to hit the sales this year and relieve the stress for next year. Talking about stress, let's take the pressure out of gift wrapping by organizing all the supplies we need to do the job creatively and quickly.

The perfect tool to help the busy woman out of the gift wrapping dilemma is a "Perfect Gift Wrap Organizer." (This can be purchased mail order. See information on page 296.)

This organizer is the center of your wrapping experience and should include the tools needed to wrap those instant gifts. So begin to collect the following products:

- Shelf paper
- Wallpaper
- Newspaper—funnies, sports page, stock market section, travel section
- Fabric
- Tissue paper—white (great for rubber-stamping), colors, plain, pin-dot, graph, or patterned
- Gift boxes—enameled, fold-up, acrylic, or Lucite
- Gift bags and totes—lunch bags, enamel bags, cellophane bags, window bags, small bottle and jar bags
- Tags or enclosure cards
- Ribbon—satin, plaid, taffeta, curling ribbon, curly satin, fabric, rickrack, shoelaces, measuring tape, lace, jute
- Stickers
- Mailing labels
- Glue gun, glue sticks

- Chenille stems—use on your make-ahead bows and store in a Perfect box
- Rubber stamps, stamp pad, or brush markers

Hints for Use of Old Wrapping Paper and Bows

- Make used wrapping paper new again by lightly spraying the wrong side with spray starch and pressing with a warm iron.
- Run wrinkled ribbon through a hot curling iron to take out old creases. I keep an old one in my "Perfect Gift Wrap Organizer."
- Ribbons—Make your own with pieces of leftover fabric. Almost any type of fabric can be cut to the desired width and length. Striped materials are great to cut into even widths. Press fabric strips between sheets of wax paper with a hot iron. This will keep the strips from unraveling and provide enough stiffness for the ribbon to hold its shape when making it into a bow.

More Wrapping Ideas

Cellophane
- For those "How am I going to wrap that?" gifts. It will always get you out of a jam.
- For a basket, bucket, pail, or small wagon toy filled with goodies—tied with a fluffy bow and a sprig of holly or pine, or decorative stickers.
- For your gifts of food—cookies on a Christmas plate, breads wrapped with cellophane and Christmas ribbon, a homemade quiche, a basket of muffins in a checked napkin or muffins in a muffin tin.
- For a plant.
- For fresh bouquet of flowers—tied with a beautiful bow and a special note inside.

Gift Bags
A wonderful idea for a quick, easy, and decorative way to wrap! They are reusable too!

Line bag with contrasting tissue or wrap your gift item or items in tissue. Add a bow to the handle with a gift tag. Add Tissue Toss on top for a festive look. (Tissue Toss: Use any color combination of tissue depending on the time of the year. Cut tissue into 1/4-inch strips, then toss like a green salad and you've made Tissue Toss.)

Decorate bag with stickers, banners, or cutouts from old Christmas cards.

Large silver or black or green plastic garbage bags may be just the thing to hide a large gift. Add a banner, large bow, and stickers. It will look just like Santa's pack. Reuse your bags for lunches or to hold your needlework.

Gift Boxes and Containers
- The decorated ones need only a ribbon! Always get a courtesy box, tissue, and ribbon whenever you buy anything at a department store or where the gift wrap is free. Save them in your gift wrap center for the times you need them. Usually they fold flat and are easy to store.
- Wrap a lid separate from the bottom to use again and again.
- Use tins, ceramic containers, Lucite or acrylic boxes, flowerpots, buckets, pails, and baskets.

Gift Certificates
- Purchase from stores
- Make your own with calligraphy, sticker art, or rubber-stamp art and then laminate them. Have certificates redeemable for:

Babysitting	Day of shopping and lunch
Dinners in your home	Trip to the zoo
Frozen yogurt	Plays

These ideas should help to stimulate your creative juices in making the gift wrapping in your life a happy, pleasant experience.

Foods and Kitchen

How to Save Money at the Supermarket

> Plans fail for lack of counsel, but with many advisers they succeed.
> —*Proverbs 15:22 NIV*

*T*ODAY in our busy society we find that much of our stress is caused by how we provide nutrition for our family. At one time in our society there was much emphasis upon the family spending quality time around the dining room table. Many times in years gone by we could expect to have at least two of the three meals (breakfast and dinner) together. The dinner table was a great place to have a "summit conference" or just to catch up on the day's happenings.

Today with our hustled, hassled, and hurried society, we have stopped or seriously neglected this tradition. I encourage each family to seriously evaluate their family time and see if at least one meal can be shared together. If you do make this commitment, try to make the meal a pleasant time for the family. You want it to be a rewarding experience. This is not the time to be negative. Make it an uplifting time, one where everyone will go away wanting to get back together again.

Many busy families have surrendered to the fast-food phenomenon and very rarely cook at home. This is fine occasionally but should be viewed cautiously for regular meals. Those who find themselves on tight budgets will soon find the fast-food compromise most expensive. In many cases, it also deprives your family of balanced nutrition.

Don't view food preparation as drudgery, but delight in providing meals for your family. There are excellent cookbooks available that simplify food preparation. To ease your planning you might make up 3 x 5 cards giving you about seven different recipes for breakfast, lunch, and dinner. By rotating the cards, you can have variety and not get bored with your meals. Try to introduce a new recipe occasionally. If you have teenagers, they can be of great assistance. They can set the table, shop, clean vegetables, start the meal, serve the food, clean the table, and even load the dishwasher (if you have one). This is an excellent opportunity to teach your children many lessons for the adult life: meal planning, shopping for bargains, budget preparation, nutritional balance, table etiquette, time management in cooking meals, and meal cleanup.

I have a friend who took one summer to teach her teenage sons how to survive—she called it "Survival Summer." At the end of the summer she felt comfortable and self-assured that her boys could take care of themselves in an emergency. An added benefit is that she now has help to relieve her of her expanding responsibilities.

One word of caution is that busy teenagers carrying a heavy college-prep academic load must have time for the studies; however, this doesn't mean that they don't carry some responsibilities for family functions.

To help you save money at the supermarket I have listed several helpful hints for you. These should not only make shopping more efficient, but also save you some money.

1. *Shop with a purpose and with a list.* Plan your menus for the entire week (or two) and then organize your shopping list so that you have to pass through each section of the supermarket only once. You might even make a list of standard products, arranged to correspond to the flow of your normal supermarket. (See page 174 for a sample of a marketing list.) If you have to return to the first aisle to pick up just one thing, you may find yourself attracted by other items. This will push you over your food budget and cause you added stress.

2. *Try to control your impulse buying.* Studies have estimated that almost 50 percent of purchases are entirely unplanned (not on your list). Be especially careful at the start of your shopping trip when your cart is nearly empty. You're more susceptible to high-priced, unplanned purchases then.

3. *Get your shopping done within a half hour.* This means you don't shop during rush hour. Shopping at busy times will hurry you up, and you will have a greater tendency to just pull items from the shelves without really shopping comparatively for the best product. Supermarkets are often very comfortable places to linger, but one study suggests that customers spend at least 75 cents a minute after a half-hour in the store.

4. *Shop alone if you can.* Children and even dads can cause you to compromise from your lists as they try to help you with unplanned purchases. Television advertising can cause great stress when your children go with you. They want to make sure they have the latest cereal, even though it is loaded with sugar and has very little nutritional value.

5. *Never shop when hungry.* Enough said. The psychology is obvious.

6. *Use coupons wisely.* Food companies often use coupon offers to promote either new products or old products that haven't been selling well. Ask yourself if you would have bought the item had there been no coupon, and compare prices with competing brands to see if you're really saving money.

7. *Be a smart shopper.* Be aware that grocery stores stock the highest-priced items at eye level. The lower-priced staples like flour, sugar, and salt are often below eye level, as are bulk quantities of many items. More and more specialty stores are carrying bulk food, which can give you excellent cost savings if you are buying for a large family or joint-purchasing for several families or even for a picnic. One word of caution is that even though you might save money on bulk buying, you might really spend more because your family doesn't consume the item fast enough; you find that it spoils and you end up throwing away excess. This can be expensive and not a savings. Also, be aware that foods displayed at the end of an aisle may appear to be on sale, but often are not.

8. *Use unit pricing.* Purchase a small, inexpensive pocket calculator to take with you to the market. This way you can divide the price or the item by the number of units in the package to find the cost per unit. This way you can compare apples with apples. The lowest-priced container does not always have the cheapest price per unit.

9. *Avoid foods that are packaged as individual servings.* Extra packaging usually boosts the price of the product. This becomes too expensive for families. In some cases a one- or two-member family might be able to buy in this portion; however, for the general buying

of American families you would not find this an economical way to purchase food.

10. *When buying meat consider the amount of lean meat in the cut as well as the price per pound.* A relatively high-priced cut with little or no waste may provide more meat for your money than a low-priced cut with a great deal of bone, gristle, or fat. Chicken, turkey, and fish are often good bargains for the budget buyer.

11. *Buy vegetables and fruits in season* since they'll be at their peak of quality and their lowest price. Never buy the first crop; prices are sure to go down. You might even want to consider planning an "old-time canning weekend." Canning produce yourself gives you the greatest economy and lets you enjoy these delicacies all during the year.

As an informed consumer you need to become more and more aware of what the labels on your products mean. Remember that manufacturers have to add additives and preservatives to give color and longer shelf-life to their products. As a buyer you may not be willing to make that trade-off. There are a lot of natural foods on the market and these can certainly help protect your family from the side effects of additives. Labels can tip you off to what's in the jar or the carton, so it's wise to know how to read them.

What Food Labels Tell You

• *Ingredients.* Ingredients must be listed in descending order of prominence by weight. The first ingredients listed are the main ingredients in that product.

• *Colors and flavors.* Added colors and flavors do not have to be listed by name, but the use of artificial colors or flavors must be indicated.

• *Serving content.* For each serving: the serving size; the number of calories per serving; the amount of protein, carbohydrates, and fat in a serving; the percentage of the U.S. Recommended Daily Allowance (USRDA) for protein and seven important vitamins and minerals.

• *Optional information.* Some labels also contain the following: the percentage of the USRDA for any of 12 additional vitamins and minerals: the amount of saturated and unsaturated fat and cholesterol in a serving; and the amount of sodium furnished by a serving.

What Food Labels Don't Tell You

• *What standardized foods contain.* Over 350 foods, including common ones like enriched white bread and catsup, are classified as "standardized." The Food and Drug Administration (FDA) has established guidelines for these products and manufacturers are therefore not required to list ingredients.

• *How much sugar is in some products.* Sugar and sweeteners come in a variety of forms (white sugar, brown sugar, corn syrup, dextrose, sucrose, maltose, corn sweeteners), and if they're all listed separately, it's nearly impossible to know the true amount of sugar contained in a labeled product.

• *How "natural" a product is.* The FDA's policy on using the word "natural" on a food label is loose. The product may, in fact, be highly processed and full of additives.

• *Specific ingredients that may be harmful.* Because coloring or spices that don't have to be listed by name can cause nausea, dizziness, or hives in certain people, people with food or additive allergies may have trouble knowing which products they need to avoid.

As an informed shopper you have more control over your purchase style and habits. Much of your budget goes to food. Become a good steward of God's money and get the most in return for it. Be knowledgeable in all phases of living.

44

Turning Coupons into Cash

Trust in your money and down you go! Trust in God and flourish as a tree!
—*Proverbs 11:28*

*M*ANY SMART WOMEN are saving money by couponing.

Today's household is certainly concerned with finances.

I've talked with several women who are a part of a coupon club in their church. They meet monthly to exchange coupons and rebate forms. These women have a well-organized file system for their coupons. They bring in magazines and newspapers given to them by other people so the time can be spent in cutting out coupons and filing away or exchanging them with each other.

I've found that an accordion 9 x 5½ file is a great tool for organizing your coupons. Your topics could include:

Personal/health	Mixes
Laundry	Frozen
Poultry/meats	Cleaners
Cereals	Baking products
Baby	Soda pop
Dairy	Dry goods

Breads	Snacks
Garden	Cookies
Charcoal	Salad seasoning
Soups	Package mixes
Sauces	Jams
Rice	Coffee/tea
Lunch meats	Miscellaneous
Paper products	

When cutting out a coupon, run a yellow highlighter pen over the expiration date. That way your eye will catch the date quickly.

I met a beautiful young mother who told me she saved $850.00 last year by couponing. Another working woman saved $1,100 couponing in one year.

These women struck my interest and I asked them to share with me some of their ideas that helped save them that kind of money. Here are some of those ideas:

• A store will run a special ad in the local newspaper; for example, coffee at $1.99. You have a coffee coupon for 50 cents off. This week you also cut out a coupon that entitles you to a double discount on any coupon. You then can purchase that $1.99 can of coffee for only 99 cents.

• Whenever possible use double coupons. If your market is not honoring double coupons, it could be worth driving to another local market that is.

• You can cut out coupons for "luxury" items (freezer baggies, an expensive brand of disposable diapers, pie crust mix, etc.) and many times end up finding these things on a clearance table, either discontinued by the market or the manufacturer, or damaged. Then, with your coupon doubled you can get it free or at a minimal price. (Homemade-type mix for rye bread, clearance priced at 90 cents, with a 40-cent doubled coupon cost me 10 cents.) On items used a lot that are costly (disposable diapers, soda pop, or coffee for some people) *drive* to another neighborhood market for a great deal. The savings are far worth it. Stock up as much as your budget and number of double coupons will allow. When a meat item is priced well, stock up on it at a different store. If you eat a lot of poultry and prefer breast meat only, go elsewhere when you can save 60 to 70 cents per pound. Because you stock up, you won't have to do this very often. Also, there are many poultry coupons available; double them for more savings.

• What is hard to understand is that in double-couponing the *smaller* quantity is usually the better buy because you can get it for a few cents, if not free. Just buy two or three dish detergents, and you'll have enough until another brand goes on special.

• Switch brands of most items regularly. Couponing lets you try lots of products. Obviously there are some things you won't care for, so don't buy them again. But on the average you can switch peanut butter, jelly, rice, margarine, coffee, soda pop, paper towels, toilet paper, etc. You might find a better product in the sampling. Because of couponing, generic is *not* always the best buy. If you can get a superior product for the same price or less, then use a coupon. Stock up on staples and paper products. (If you don't have very much storage, you can put things in the garage or even under the beds.) Most important is getting hold of coupons and filing them. Throw *nothing* away, even if you get two major papers on Thursday (or whatever day is food section day for you!) Tucked into our throwaway neighborhood advertising paper is Safeway's advertising circular. My market is currently doubling *all* other market's coupons, so I cut out Safeway's coupons and keep them for that week. Friends and neighbors can even give you leftover coupons that are mailed to them. You can use many of these as well. However, go through your file once or twice a month to discard those which have gone beyond their expiration date.

• Refunding is complicated, or can be, so you may set up rules for yourself. Get all refunding forms from newspapers or magazines because most markets don't stock them. Don't buy the required number of products *unless* you have the refund form. (It's easy to have the advertiser say the refund form is available at your grocer's, but it rarely is, unfortunately.) Try to combine your refunds with purchasing the item on sale, with a doubled coupon, or, better, both! It must be something you use often, not a new, untried product. (Who wants three boxes of terrible-tasting cereal in your cupboards with another free one on the way!) Many people save all box tops and wrappings. I've tried it and it simply was not worth it. Most refunds are for combinations of foods I don't buy or use. Therefore, wait until you see the requirements and then decide if it is worth the effort and postage.

Where can you get coupons? Many places—a lot come through the mail. I used to throw out junk mail and not even look at it. Now I quickly finger through the pages and cut the coupons—before tossing the rest.

Major and local newspapers run coupons every week.

Friends can cut coupons and save them for you. My auntie cuts coupons; it gives her a purpose to help plus any coupons she doesn't use she passes on to me, and any I don't use I then pass on to our married daughter, Jenny.

Grandmas and grandpas use couponing as a great project.

Neighbors', friends', and relatives' cast-off magazines are also a great source of coupons.

Cutting out, filing, and organizing will take you no more than a half-hour per week, and this could very well save you $13.00 to $20.00 per week on your grocery bill. This pays you four to six times minimum wage. It's fun, too, and very rewarding.

Try it—you'll love it. It's another way of being a good steward of your money.

One woman shared with me that she would write her check at the checkout stand for the total amount and then pocket her savings from coupons, thus giving her money which she spent on Christmas presents. Her husband was so excited about what she did that he told everyone how proud he was of a wife who looks well into her household, being a Proverbs 31 woman.

Remember, coupons give savings!

45

Planning Meals Saves Stress

Let each of you look out not only
for his own interests, but also for
the interests of others.

—*Philippians 2:4 NKJV*

*T*HE AVERAGE WOMAN cooks, plans, markets, chops, pares, cleans up or eats out over 750 meals a year. If this is anywhere close to true, doesn't it stand to reason this is an area we need to organize? Feeding our families certainly is a big part of our lives—not to mention feeding them with good nutrition. We will gravitate to foods that have been planned and prepared. Here are easy steps and hints to successful meals.

1. Make a simple meal-planner chart. On an 8½ x 11 sheet of paper list the days of the week. Start on the left side from top to bottom. Then across the top list "Breakfast," "Lunch," "Dinner." These will form an easy chart as you draw lines dividing each day and meal time. A sample chart (Figure 5) is included on the following page.

2. From your meal planner, make out a marketing list. Start by listing items needed as they appear on the aisles in your supermarket. This will prevent backtracking in the market. You want to get in and get out. A study showed after the first half-hour

WEEKLY MENUS

Date __Jan 7-13__

Day of week	Breakfast	Lunch	Dinner
Monday			
Tuesday	Hot cereal	Salami sandwich	Chicken
Wednesday			
Thursday	Granola + bananas	Turkey-cheese sandwich	Lasagna casserole
Friday			
Saturday	Pancakes	Turkey hot dogs	Tacos
Sunday			

Figure 5

in the market a woman will spend at least 75 cents per minute. Stick to your list and use coupons.

3. Post your meal-planner chart so all family members can see it. Should you be late arriving home, older family members can check the planner and start dinner for you.

4. Don't forget Tupper Suppers—premade meals that have been prepared ahead of time and are stored in Tupperware or containers in the freezer or refrigerator.

5. Plan family favorites into each week.

6. Remember to include things still in the freezer from previous month plan-overs or leftovers.

7. Also listed on your menu planner you can schedule which person in the family sets the table that day or week; also who clears off. Our rule was whoever set the table also cleared it off.

8. Teach creativity in setting the table by allowing each person, when it's their turn, to use paper or cloth napkins, paper or glass dishes, a candle, a few fresh flowers, Teddy Bear, a pumpkin, or whatever they think of for a centerpiece.

9. To quickly remove water from the lettuce greens that you have just washed, simply put into a clean pillowcase or lingerie bag and spin in your washing machine for two minutes. Remove from the bag and tear lettuce, making a big salad. Store in refrigerator for up to two weeks.

10. Make up your own TV dinners. Use containers purchased in your market for microwave or regular ovens. Then put your leftovers in sections of the trays and freeze. Great for dad and children when mom's away.

11. Keep parsley fresh and crisp. Wash the parsley and put a bunch of sprigs into a jar, stem ends down. Pour in an inch or two of cold water, enough for the stems to stand in without the leaves touching the water. Tighten the lid, set the jar in the refrigerator, and enjoy crisp parsley for up to two weeks.

12. To speed up baking potatoes, simply put a clean nail through the potato. It will cook in half the time.

13. A piece of lettuce dropped into a pot of soup will soak up the excess grease. Remove the lettuce as soon as it has absorbed the grease.

14. Our family loves BLT (bacon, lettuce, and tomato) sandwiches. Whenever I fry or microwave bacon, I cook a few extra

pieces and put them into a plastic freezer bag and freeze. They are ready for the next BLT sandwich.

15. Leftover pancakes or waffles? Don't discard them—pop them into the toaster or oven for a quick and easy breakfast or afterschool snack.

16. For the two of us I bake six large potatoes. We eat them baked the first night. The second serving is sliced and fried in a bit of butter. The last two potatoes are cubed and served in a cream sauce with some cheese.

17. To get more juice out of a lemon, place it in a microwave oven for 30 seconds. Squeeze the lemon and you will get twice as much juice. Vitamins won't be destroyed.

18. Frozen foods have a definite freezer life; it is important to use the food within the specified period of time. The easiest way to mark meat and other frozen foods is to put a "use by" date on a label or on the package. Your market does this and it makes good sense.

19. Freeze lunchbox sandwiches. They can be made up by the week. Put on all the ingredients except lettuce. It will save time and trouble.

20. You can make your own convenience foods. Chop large batches of onion, green pepper, or nuts, and freeze them in small units. Grate a week's or month's worth of cheese, then freeze it in recipe-size portions. Shape ground meat or ground turkey into patties so you can thaw a few at a time. Freeze homemade casseroles, soups, stews, and chilies in serving-size portions for faster thawing and reheating.

21. No need to boil those lasagna noodles anymore! Just spread sauce in the bottom of the pan, place hard, uncooked noodles on top and spread sauce on top of noodles. Continue with the other layers, finishing with noodles and sauce. Cover with foil and bake at 350 degrees for 1 hour and 15 minutes. This will probably be the best hint you'll ever get.

22. Before freezing fresh bagels, cut them in half. When you're ready to use them, they will defrost faster and can even be toasted while they are still frozen.

23. Fruit prepared ahead of time will keep well if you squeeze lemon juice over it and refrigerate. The juice of half a lemon is enough for up to two quarts of cut fruit.

By spending a little time preparing your food and planning your meals, you'll save even more time for the other things you need to do.

Pantry Organization

> You must love and help your
> neighbors just as much as you love
> and take care of yourself.
>
> —*James 2:8*

*T*HE LAST TIME I visited my aunt's house, I was looking for the dry cereal one morning. "Oh, you'll find it in the pantry next to the cat food," my aunt said as she nodded her head in the direction of a colorful blue door.

I opened the door, ducking just in time to narrowly miss an avalanche of half-folded grocery sacks that came tumbling down. I wasn't as lucky with the mop handle which bopped me a good one! Buried deep in the recesses, I did manage to locate a box of Cheerios.

Although my aunt's pantry seemed more like a war zone than a pantry, your pantry can be a storehouse of confidence at your fingertips.

All it takes is some simple planning and organizing and the pantry will become your best friend.

I suggest stocking your pantry primarily with staple foods including starches, sweets, condiments, and canned or bottled items. These will last for six months or longer.

Perishable goods can also be stored in a pantry. The only difference is, of course, that they will have to be replenished more often. The chart (Figure 6) on page 174 will help you keep track of the basics.

Arranging Your Pantry

1. When stocking your pantry, organize your staples and canned goods by category. For example, put canned fruit in one row and dry cereal in another, or organize everything alphabetically.
2. To help keep your food items in the right place, label your pantry shelves accordingly. This is also on excellent way to keep your spices in order.
3. Sort your packaged items such as dry taco mix, salad dressing, and gravy mix in a large jar or small shoebox covered with contact paper.
4. Store as much as possible in jars—everything from tea bags to flour and noodles to coffee filters. Products are protected from moisture and tend to stay fresh longer when placed in jars.
5. For convenience, save one shelf for appliances and group them according to function. For example, keep your mixing bowls, mixers, and measuring cups together.
6. As you plan your weekly menus, check your staple and perishable foods and replenish if necessary.

Other Helpful Hints

• Use freezer and storage space well. If you take advantage of sales and coupons to stock up and save money, you can avoid many of those "emergency" trips to the supermarket when unexpected company arrives.
• Plan a "cooking marathon" with a friend or your family. Bake or cook a few entrees such as breads, cakes, casseroles and soups. Freeze the items, some in family portions and some in individual servings. Remember to date and label each item. Now, on a day when mom's sick or there's no time to cook a meal, you can open your freezer and take your pick!
• Make your own TV dinners by using a sectional paper plate or pie tin and adding leftovers to each section throughout the week. Then freeze the whole plate. Your kids will be able to fend for themselves on the nights you can't be home.

You'll be surprised at how a little organization in your pantry will not only save you precious time, but will relieve a potential area of stress as well.

PANTRY STOCKING LIST

Date _____

Qty.	Cost		Qty.	Cost	
		Starches	____	____	Jello
____	____	Flour	____	____	Pudding mix
____	____	Cornmeal	____	____	Soup
____	____	Oatmeal	____	____	
____	____	Pasta	____	____	
____	____	White rice	____	____	
____	____	Brown rice			
____	____	Potatoes			**Condiments**
____	____		____	____	Ketchup
____	____		____	____	Vinegar
____	____		____	____	Capers
____	____		____	____	Brown mustard
			____	____	Yellow mustard
		Sweet-based staples	____	____	Oil
____	____	Brown sugar	____	____	Tabasco sauce
____	____	White sugar	____	____	Worchestershire sauce
____	____	Powdered sugar	____	____	
____	____	Honey	____	____	
____	____	Maple syrup	____	____	
____	____	Jams/jellies			**Perishable foods**
____	____				Fresh garlic
____	____		____	____	Ginger
____	____		____	____	Green peppers
			____	____	Celery
		Canned & bottled goods	____	____	Eggs
			____	____	Nuts
____	____	Tuna	____	____	Green onions
____	____	Juices	____	____	Yellow onions
____	____	Peanut butter	____	____	White onions
____	____	Tomato sauce	____	____	Tomatoes
____	____	Tomato paste	____	____	Carrots
____	____	Dried fruit	____	____	White cheese
____	____	Dried mixes (i.e. salad dressing, taco mix)	____	____	Yellow cheese
			____	____	Lemons
____	____	Canned vegetables	____	____	
____	____	Canned fruit	____	____	
____	____	Pancake mix	____	____	

Figure 6

Kitchen Organization

Happy are those who are strong in
the Lord, who want above all else
to follow your steps.

—*Psalm 84:5*

*A*MERICAN KITCHENS are busy places. Today's women spend an average of 1,092 hours a year there, along with everyone from husbands to friends to teenagers to dinner guests to babysitters. That little room puts up with a lot of traffic, and organization is essential. But how, how, *how* do we do it?

It takes time, but it is well worth it. Organization frees you from your kitchen mess and gives you total rest in this big area of your life. Here's a plan to get you started.

What You Need

Jars (assorted sizes), covered plastic containers, lazy Susans, large cardboard box marked "kitchen overflow," contact paper, trash bag, markers, and labels. Most important, you need a two-to-three-hour slot of time and some help from your family. When family members help get the kitchen in order, they're more likely to help keep it that way.

Cupboards

Begin with the cupboard closest to the sink and methodically go around the kitchen. Take everything out of each cupboard. Wipe shelves and re-paper if necessary. Throw away or set aside anything that is not used daily or every other day. Pile the seldom-used items in the "kitchen overflow" box.

Put "prime time" equipment such as frequently used spices, glasses, dishes, and pots and pans back into the cupboards, placing seldom-used items toward the back or on the highest levels. Set broken appliances aside to be repaired or thrown away.

Overflow, such as odd vases, dishes, platters, pans, canned goods, seldom-used appliances, and camping equipment (which could be boxed separately) should be stored in the garage or basement to reduce kitchen clutter.

Gadgets and utensils such as wooden spoons, ladles, long-handled spoons, forks, and potato mashers can be stashed into a crock or ceramic pot to save space. Either sharpen dull knives or throw them out. Try a plastic divider (usually used for flatware) in the junk drawer for storing a small hammer, tacks, screwdriver, nails, batteries, glue, etc.

Pots and Pans

To keep pots and pans in neat order, try lining the shelves with plain or light-colored paper and drawing an exaggerated outline of each item. Then store each pot or pan in its designated space. You'll be surprised at how easy it will be to find things.

Refrigerator

Don't let your refrigerator intimidate you; just think of it as another closet. Store fruits and vegetables in covered plastic containers, baggies, or refrigerator drawers to insure freshness. Keep meats and cheeses on the coldest shelf, and rotate eggs so that you use the oldest first. Lazy Susans are great refrigerator space-savers and can be used to hold sour cream, cottage cheese, jellies, peanut butter, mustard, and whatever else is cluttering up your refrigerator. You can also buy dispensers and bottle racks which attach to refrigerator shelves.

Freezer

The cardinal rule for freezer organization is to date and label *everything*. Be sure to avoid mystery packages! Shape hamburger into patties, freeze on a cookie sheet, and then transfer to plastic bags. They won't stick together and will thaw quickly for meatloaf, burgers, tacos, casseroles, or spaghetti. Keep ahead of ice cubes by periodically bagging up a bunch. Frozen packaged vegetables go together in the freezer as do ice cream and frozen desserts. Potato chips, corn chips, nuts, breads, muffins, wheat flour, and tortillas (corn and flour), even candies, all freeze well. Your freezer can be a real time-saver if you make dinners ahead. Lasagna, noodle and cheese casseroles, soups, beans, spaghetti sauce, and enchiladas are yummy freeze-ahead meals. If you're freezing in jars, be sure to leave $1\frac{1}{2}$ inches at the top for expansion.

Planning Your Kitchen

I will reject all selfishness and stay away from every evil. I will not tolerate anyone who secretly slanders his neighbors.

—Psalm 101:4,5

$\mathcal{A}$ WELL-PLANNED KITCHEN is the envy of all those whose kitchens are an obstacle course to efficient cooking. No matter how large or small, any kitchen can be tailored to suit your lifestyle if thought is given to your cooking habits and needs.

Here are some helps for a well-planned kitchen.

1. Invest in a good selection of pans and utensils to accomplish your culinary pursuits. These should include:

- One 10-inch skillet w/lid
- One 8-to 10-inch omelet pan
- A set of covered casserole dishes
- A roasting pan with rack
- Bread pans
- Two cookie sheets
- Double boiler
- One muffin pan with 6 to 12 cups
- Dutch oven or similar type of pan

Basic Utensils

Begin with a good set of knives. Bob and I have been married almost 35 years and just this year we invested in knives. This should have been done years ago. These items are all great ideas for shower and wedding gifts for the bride and groom. Be sure to include a steel knife sharpener for proper maintenance of your knife set investment.

Other Necessary Items for the Kitchen

- A set of measuring cups
- Wooden spoons—a variety of sizes.
- A mallet for tenderizing less expensive cuts of meat.
- Spatula—I like the rubber type.
- Shears—great for cutting parsley, green onions and meat.
- Rolling pin
- Storage bowls (such as Tupperware)
- Cleaner
- Cheese slicer
- Tongs
- Garlic press—I use this often.

Gadgets

- Grater
- Colander
- Sifter
- Vegetable steamer
- Food grinder
- Eggbeater
- Whisk
- Egg slicer—makes pretty slices for salads.

Optional Larger Gadgets

- Mixer
- Blender
- Food processor
- Toaster oven
- Microwave oven
- Freezer

2. Plan a logical work space for yourself and be sure that all utensils have a definite place. For example, if you bake a lot, set up a

baking center. It could be on the counter top near a convenient cupboard, or even on a mobile kitchen worktable.

Your mixer, baking pans, utensils, and canisters should be readily accessible to that area.

Things That Work Together Should Be Stored Together. This is a good rule to remember when organizing your kitchen. Think through your daily work pattern and plan your space accordingly.

Items seldom used, such as a turkey platter, deviled egg dish, roasting pan, seasonal tableware, serving dishes, and picnic gear should be kept on higher shelves.

If you get a new set of flatware, keep the old to use for parties or to loan out when friends have buffets or church socials.

Spices can be retrieved quickly if stored in alphabetical order: Store on a "lazy Susan" or have your helpful handyman make a wooden spice rack to hang on your wall.

Here's a cute idea for that bridal shower. Have each guest bring (or tie on the top of their package) a spice. Specify a name brand so the spices will be uniform. You could even specify the type of spice on the invitation to prevent repetition.

Use a crock to store your utensils; place on the stove for quick retrieval. It's also a space saver that can take the place of a drawer. It can include your wooden spoons, whisks, meat mallet, ladles, and spatula.

Appliances

The many compact appliances available today are perfect for newlyweds looking to use time and space in the kitchen efficiently.

Mini food-processors and compact mincer-choppers, for instance, are suited for cooking meals for two or three people and are easier to clean than their full counterparts. They also take less space and less time.

Toaster ovens are handy for small meals. To save space they can be mounted under a cabinet. Rechargeable, hand-held beaters can be mounted on the wall. And some new coffee makers on the market brew a single mug at a time.

Several factors should be considered with purchasing appliances:

• Space: If you are short on counter space, look at undercabinet models.

• Convenience: Look for cordless products. They rest in a recharger base and are always ready to use.

• Weight comfort: Make sure hand-held appliances such as mixers and cordless knives are lightweight and easy to grip.

• Ease of operation: Push-button controls simplify use. Certain controls, such as a pulse control, regulate the amount of processing.

• Automatic shutoff: For peace of mind and for added safety, look for appliances that shut off automatically, including irons and coffee makers.

• Dishwasher safety: For maximum convenience, look for products with parts that can be easily disassembled and put into the dishwasher.

Other Handy Tips

• Glue a 12-inch square of cork to the inside of the cabinet door over your kitchen work area. On the cork tack the recipe card you are using and newspaper clippings of recipes you plan to try within a few days. It keeps them at eye level and they stay spatter-free.

• When using your electric can opener, help save your fingers from cuts by placing a refrigerator magnet on top of the can before opening it. This magnet will give you a good grip when you lift off the lid.

• Increase your efficiency with an extra-long phone cord that will reach to all corners of your kitchen. Instead of wasting time while on the phone, you can cook, set the table, or clean out a drawer. A speaker phone provides similar freedom.

• Meat slices easier if it's partially frozen.

• Want to mix frozen juice in a hurry without using the blender? Use your potato masher on the concentrate.

• You can peel garlic cloves faster if you mash them lightly with the side of the blade of a chef's knife.

• To keep bugs out of your flour canister, put a stick of spearmint gum in the flour and it will stay bug-free.

• Mark your bowls and their covers with the same number, using a marking pencil. Then you won't always be looking for a matching cover for the bowl when you're putting away leftovers. All you have to do is match the numbers.

• Arrange your kitchen for maximum efficiency. Position often-used utensils in convenient drawers and cupboards. Make your dishes do double duty. Use a saucepan as mixing bowl; then use the same pan for the cooking.

• Cut the lid off an egg carton and place the cups in a kitchen drawer. You can organize your cup hooks, small nails, paper clips, thumbtacks, and other small items. No more junky drawers.

• When you are in need of extra ice cubes for party or summer use, simply fill your egg cartons with water and freeze.

• If wax has built up on the felt pads of your floor polisher, place the pads between several thicknesses of paper toweling and press with a warm iron. The towels will quickly absorb the old wax.

• Place the plastic lids from coffee cans under bottles of cooking oil to keep cabinets clean. When the lids get dirty, just throw them away.

• A rubber jar-opener (or rubber gloves) gives you easy access to anything in a tightly closed jar.

• To cover kitchen cabinet shelves, apply easy-to-install vinyl floor squares by just peeling off the backing. They are particularly good for lower shelves where pots and pans are usually stored. They cut easily and do not tear or wrinkle.

• One of the best appliances you can have for your busy schedule is a slow cooker (crockpot). Prepare the meal early in the morning and when you come home from shopping or work, you will find your main dish for dinner ready.

• At least once a year pull the plug on your refrigerator and give it a thorough cleaning. Rinse with clean water after cleaning with baking soda (one tablespoon baking soda to one quart water). Let it air-dry.

• A trash can under the kitchen sink takes up some very valuable storage space. Take a large decorative basket and line it with a plastic bag. The bag is easy to lift out when full. Train several family members to take the trash out.

Remember, your kitchen is for *cooking,* not clutter!

49

Eggs, Eggs, and More Eggs

I will also meditate on all Your
work, and talk of Your deeds.
—*Psalm 77:12* NKJV

*S*UE GREGG and I in our book *Eating Right* (Harvest House) wrote a chapter dealing with the misunderstanding about eggs in our diet. The controversy and confusion over eggs focuses on the high cholesterol content of egg yolks. Media advertising, news articles, magazines, nutrition books, cookbooks, doctors, and nutritionists would have us believe that food cholesterol raises blood cholesterol. Yet there is no adequate research to substantiate this claim. Researchers are not agreed at all on this issue. The classic study that relates egg yolk cholesterol to blood cholesterol was conducted in 1913 by Nikolai Anichkov, a Russian pathologist, on rabbits. He fed rabbits the equivalent in human consumption of 60 eggs per day. The rabbits developed cholesterol deposits on their arteries. But rabbits are total vegetarians and do not eat eggs. There is nothing in their metabolism to handle eggs.

No human study shows a clear relationship between food cholesterol content and blood cholesterol, whereas research does indicate a clearer relationship to total fat consumption, especially to saturated fat. Yet eggs are lower in saturated fat than both meat and poultry, about the same as lowfat yogurt, and contain one-third of the amount that is in 1/4 cup of cheddar cheese.

Advertising and popular news articles repeatedly reinforce the notion that food cholesterol raises blood cholesterol levels. "No cholesterol" labels are printed on vegetable oils and advertised everywhere. The message is effectively communicated, "Cholesterol in foods must be bad!"

Time magazine, March 26, 1984, reported the most extensive research project ever conducted on cholesterol in medical history. This project was declared "... a turning point in cholesterol-heart disease research," because it clearly demonstrated that high blood cholesterol contributes to heart disease and cardiac deaths. Ten years and $150 million were spent on 3,806 men, ages 35 to 39 with cholesterol levels of 265 milligrams. A cholesterol-lowering drug was used in the study. Those receiving the drug experienced an 8.5 percent drop in cholesterol, 19 percent fewer heart attacks, and 24 percent fewer cardiac deaths. Yet nothing was changed in their diets. The study had nothing to do with the cholesterol content of any foods.

The editors of *Time* magazine placed a "sad-face" picture on the front cover of this same issue, using two fried eggs for eyes and a slice of bacon for the mouth, with the overcaption: "Cholesterol . . . And Now the Bad News." The article was titled, "Hold the Eggs and Butter" (page 56). The message conveyed to the reader was "Eggs and butter contribute to heart disease." Yet the research project reviewed by *Time* had nothing to do with the effects of food on cholesterol! This kind of media influence confuses important nutritional issues of the American public. Of this research project Edward Ahrens, researcher at Rockefeller University, said, "Since this was basically a drug study we can conclude nothing about diet; such extrapolation is unwarranted, unscientific and wishful thinking" (*Time* magazine, March 26, 1984, page 58).

Only 20 to 30 percent of our cholesterol comes from food. Our bodies manufacture the rest. There are many other influences on blood cholesterol levels besides total fat intake, such as exercise, stress, inherited genes, prepackaged foods high in fats and refined carbohydrates, lack of dietary fiber, and inadequate vitamins and minerals. Rather than focus on egg yolks as a dietary disaster, we should develop a balance of real whole foods.

Eggs are a real food. They can readily be used in baking and a couple of times a week for meals. Two breakfasts or an egg main dish will not raise the total fat intake to over 30 percent of daily calories. Eggs are our best protein source because their amino acid pattern most nearly matches that needed for human growth and health. They are excellent sources of trace minerals; unsaturated fatty acids; iron; phosphorus; vitamin B-complex; and vitamins A, E, K, and even some D. Most of these reside in the egg yolk! Yolks also are the highest food source of choline, a component of lecithin that assists in keeping cholesterol liquid in the bloodstream. There is some question as to whether the lecithin is effective in this way, however.

If you do not want to eat egg yolks or are allergic to eggs, be encouraged. There are easy alternatives! You can use two egg whites in place of a whole egg in almost any baking recipe. Unfortunately that wastes the egg yolks, so we prefer using 1/4 cup tofu in place of an egg. Mixing it in the blender with other liquid ingredients works best. If you cannot find a real food to give taste pleasure, we recommend doing without.

Consider the value of fertile eggs. Fertile eggs come from hens, living with roosters, that are allowed to grow and peck on the ground. They receive no drugs as chickens raised in close quarters do. We don't really know what the nutritional difference between fertile eggs and sterile eggs is even though some people make claims for the nutritional superiority of fertile eggs. The clearest advantage is that fertile eggs are free of chemical residues. In general, fertile eggs also taste fresher but are also slightly more expensive. Many health food stores carry them. People who raise their own chickens also often sell them.

Mankind has eaten eggs for centuries. Even Job ate eggs: ". . . is there flavor in the white of an egg! I refuse to touch it; such food makes me ill" (Job 6:6,7 NIV). Yet heart disease was not reported in scientific literature until 1986. You decide. We still believe eggs are an economical blessing from God given to us to enjoy in moderation.

Organization

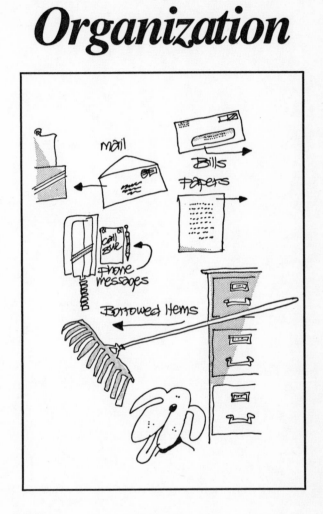

50

Telephone Tips to Give You More Time for Yourself

Set your affection on the things
above, not on things on the earth.
—*Colossians 3:2 KJV*

*H*OW MANY times have you been stuck on the telephone trying to get off but unable to end the conversation? How often have you been put on hold for what seemed like an eternity and sometimes by people who have called *you*? How many times have you finally gotten a good start on a project at home or work only to be interrupted by a telephone call you really didn't want to take?

Our telephone can be a terrific time-saver. However, it also can rule our lives if we allow calls to interrupt meals or delay departures, causing late schedules, missed appointments, etc.

Here are some tips to help you control the telephone so it doesn't control you.

1. Organize a telephone center so you can make and receive calls efficiently. Next to every phone in your home or business should be a pad and pen. Keep extra pads in a drawer or on a shelf and pencils and/or pens too. It's amazing how they wander off, so a supply is important. Your calendar, phone book, area-code map and personal address book also needs to be close by for easy reference.

2. Organize your calls so that you can make several calls at one sitting when possible. You'll be apt to make your calls shorter and get more done. List your calls, questions to ask, and points to be discussed. Date your calls and take notes for future reference. I have a personal code by each call. If the party I'm calling is not home or there's no answer I put an "O"; if the line is busy I put a wavy line. If I leave a message to call back I put a jagged line. Make up your own code that will work for you.

3. Learn how to end conversations. Getting off the phone can truly be an art. Some people ignore all the signals you give and just keep talking. To free yourself more quickly, warn people in advance that your time is limited. For example, "Your trip sounds exciting but I've got to leave in five minutes, can you tell me briefly?" Or you might insert this, "Before we hang up. . . ." It is a reminder that your call will end soon. You might say, "I really can't spend a lot of time on the phone. Let's speak briefly and meet for lunch (coffee, tea) instead."

4. The investment of an answering machine will be money well spent. You can receive calls when you're away and return calls at your convenience. Some messages will be left as reminders of appointments with no return call needed. You can also screen calls, and if it is urgent you can answer it. If not, return the call later. You can also turn on the machine while showering, bathing the baby, eating meals, doing homework, or 15 minutes before you must leave for an appointment. That way you won't be delayed by any last-minute calls that can wait.

5. If you don't have an answering machine, enlist your husband or an older child to answer the phone for an afternoon or evening when you need a block of uninterrupted time.

6. Turn off the phone or unplug it when you don't want to be disturbed during dinnertime, special projects, sewing, ironing, or family meetings.

7. Avoid phone tag. When you leave a message for someone to call you, give a time when you'll be available. If you have to get back to people, ask them when they are able to receive calls.

8. When leaving messages give as much information as possible so you can eliminate another call.

9. Return phone calls. You'll build credibility as you do.

10. If you have children take messages for you, ask them to repeat names and numbers back to callers to be sure the information is taken correctly.

11. Put a long extension cord on your telephone or consider buying a cordless phone. You will then be free to move about, clean a

bathroom, check on children, etc. This can help you do two things at once.

Using these ideas will help you to do your work more efficiently and enable you to have more hours in your day to do some things you really enjoy doing.

51

15 Minutes a Day and You're on Your Way

Seek first the kingdom of God and
His righteousness, and all these
things shall be added to you.

—*Matthew 6:33 NKJV*

*O*NE OF THE number one frustrations facing all women—single, married, career, homemakers, college students—is how we can get organized enough to eliminate all the mess within our four walls, regardless how little or large those four walls are.

Who wants to spend all their waking hours cleaning their home? Is there a way to live after a messy house? Yes. You don't have to be a slave to your home. Give me at least 15 minutes a day for five weeks and I can have you on top of the pile.

As with any task, you need some basic equipment:
• 3 large 30-gallon trash bags
• 3 to 12 large cardboard boxes (approximately 10 x 12 x 16) preferably with lids
• 1 wide-tip black felt marking pen

You might ask, where do I find these materials? Check with your local stationery store. In some cases your market has leftover boxes of some sort to get you started. Try to have all the boxes uniform in size.

Before you start this project, commit it unto the Lord. Matthew 6:33 is a good verse for this phase of the program. Ask the Lord to provide you with the desire and energy to complete the project. In this program you will clean one room a week for five weeks. If you have fewer rooms it will take you less time and if you have a larger house it will take more than five weeks.

Step 1

Start by marking the three large trash bags as follows:
• Put Away
• Throw Away
• Give Away

Step 2

Start at the front door and go through your whole house. Start with the hall closet and proceed through the living room, dining room, bedrooms, and bathrooms. End in your kitchen because you need all the experience you can get to clean that room.

Step 3

For each room's closets, drawers, and shelves you are to wash, scrub, paint, and repaper everything. Take everything out of and off of these areas and clean thoroughly.

A close friend is a great help at this point in assisting you in deciding what to throw away. Try not to become emotionally attached to any items.

A good rule to help you decide whether to keep an item is if you haven't used it for a year, it must be thrown away, given away, or stored away. Exceptions to this would be treasured keepsakes, photos, or very special things you'll want to pass down to your children someday.

Magazines, papers, scrap material, clothing, and extra dishes and pans must go.

As you pull these items off your shelves and out of your closets, they can be put into the appropriately labeled trash bags. What's left will be put back into the proper closet or drawer, or onto the proper shelf.

After the last room is finished, you will have at least three very fat trash bags.

• The *Throw Away* bag goes out to the trash area for pickup.

• The *Give Away* bag can be sorted out, divided up among needy friends, or given to a thrift store, relatives, or the Salvation Army.

• The *Put Away* bag will be the most fun of all. Take the large cardboard boxes and begin to use them for storage of the items you'll want to save for future use. (See Chapter 5 for a refresher on how to label and store these boxes.)

Just *15 minutes a day* for five weeks has cleaned out all the clutter in your home!

Maintaining Your Five-Week Program

> The Holy Spirit helps us with our
> daily problems and in our praying.
> For we don't even know what we
> should pray for.
> —*Romans 8:26*

*Y*OU NOW HAVE your home clean—washed, dusted, sorted out, and painted through this Five-Week Program—and it feels good. Everything has a place in a cupboard, dresser, closet, or on a shelf; all your boxes are marked and properly filed away. Within a short time you can locate anything. Oh, that feels good. The pressure is off!

It's a big accomplishment, but you're not quite through. It's a matter of maintaining what you've worked so hard on the past five weeks. This is the easiest part when applied.

For this phase of your program you will need:
- One 3 x 5 file box
- 36 lined 3 x 5 file cards
- Seven divider tabs

Step 1

Set-up your 3 x 5 file box with dividers.

Step 2

Label the dividers in the file box as follows:
1. Daily
2. Weekly
3. Monthly
4. Quarterly
5. Biannually
6. Annually
7. Storage (You will already have done this from a previous chapter.)

Step 3

Under each tab heading you now make a list of the jobs needing to be done on each file card. Some suggestions are:

A. *Daily*
   1. Wash dishes
   2. Make beds
   3. Sweep kitchen floor
   4. Pick up rooms
   5. Tidy bathrooms
   6. Make meal preparations, etc.

   Note: After a very short time these will become automatic and you won't need to write them down.

B. *Weekly*
   1. Monday—wash
   2. Tuesday—iron, water house plants
   3. Wednesday—mop floor, dust
   4. Thursday—vacuum, marketing
   5. Friday—change bed linens
   6. Saturday—yard work
   7. Sunday—church, free

   Note: If you skip a job on the allotted day, *DO NOT DO IT*. Skip it until the next scheduled time and put that card behind the proper tab in the file. You may have an item listed under two or more days.

C. *Monthly*
   Week 1—Clean refrigerator; clean bathrooms
   Week 2—Clean oven; wash living room windows
   Week 3—Mend clothing; wash bedroom windows
   Week 4—Clean and dust baseboards; wax kitchen floor

D. *Quarterly*
   1. Clean dresser drawers
   2. Clean out closets
   3. Move living room furniture and vacuum underneath
   4. Clean china cabinet glass
   5. Clean, rearrange, and organize cupboards in kitchen
E. *Biannually*
   1. Hose off screens
   2. Change filter in furnace
   3. Rearrange furniture
   4. Clean garage, basement, or attic (schedule the whole family on this project)
F. *Annually*
   1. Wash shear curtains
   2. Clean drapes if needed
   3. Shampoo carpet
   4. Wash walls and woodwork
   5. Paint chips or blisters on house

The above schedule is only a sample. Your particular projects can be inserted where needed. Living in different sections of our country will put different demands on your maintenance schedule. Get in the habit of staying on top of your schedule so you don't get buried again with your clutter and stress.

53

A Place
for Everything

I will trust and not be afraid, for
the Lord is my strength and song;
he is my salvation.

—*Isaiah 12:2*

CRAFT AND sewing projects are fun hobbies, but if you've dabbled in them at all you've probably struggled with where and how to store patterns, leftover fabric, straw flowers, glue, and other odds and ends.

Before you let this clutter overwhelm you, try these simple organizational hints:

• Begin collecting storage boxes such as shoe boxes, cardboard boxes, or Perfect boxes. (Perfect storage boxes are available from More Hours In My Day—see order information at back of book.)

Other containers that will work well for storing your craft items are plastic bins or stacking trays, laundry baskets, and small jars (baby food jars are great).

• Store patterns in boxes organized according to sizes and types: play clothes, dressy outfits, costumes, sportswear, blouses, and pants. Many fabric stores carry cardboard boxes made specifically for storing patterns, and you can buy these boxes at a very low price.

• Put fabrics in piles according to colors (prints, solids, and stripes) or types (wools, linens, and polyesters). Then place each pile in a separate cardboard Perfect box and number your boxes 1, 2, 3, 4, etc.

Make out a 3 x 5 file card and list on the card what type of fabric you stored in your Perfect box. On top of the card write the same number that is on the box. For example:

Box 1—Calico fabrics—reds and pinks

Box 2—Solid fabrics—blues, browns, blacks

Box 3—Stripes, polka dots

Box 4—Remnants and a yard or less of scraps

This can also be done with art and craft items. By keeping your 3 x 5 cards in a recipe box, you can quickly retrieve any item simply by looking up its card and finding the corresponding box.

• Organize buttons by color or size by stringing them onto safety pins, pipe cleaners, or plastic twist ties, or stick loose buttons and snaps on strips of transparent tape.

• Store bias tape, piping, and hem tape in a labeled shoebox.

• Keep hooks-and-eyes and snaps in baby food jars and line them up on a shelf or store them in shoe boxes, again labeled accordingly.

• String your sewing machine bobbins on pipe cleaners or keep them in a plastic ice cube tray (specialty bobbin boxes are also available at most fabric stores or drugstores).

• Organize spools of thread by grouping the spools according to color and laying them on their sides in the lids of shoe boxes. Stack the box tops so that frequently used colors are on top and stick them into a drawer or onto a shelf.

• Store fabric fill, stuffing, quilting materials, and straw or silk flowers in cardboard or Perfect boxes by using the numbering system.

• Use egg cartons for other odds and ends such as pins, small craft items, paper clips, and stamps.

• Clamp pattern pieces together with a clothespin until you finish the project or garment and then return them to the envelope.

• Large envelopes are also a great way to organize small items. The contents can be listed on the outside and stored in Perfect boxes or in a drawer. Suggested items to store are small scraps of fabric, ribbons, pipe cleaners, lace, bias tape, elastic, zippers, and stencils.

• Baskets are a fun way to store art and craft materials such as pin cushions and pins, scissors, measuring tape, ribbons, lace, and elastic.

The above items could be put into one basket and given as a gift to a creative craft friend for Christmas.

Another cute idea is to spray-glue one of the Perfect storage boxes and apply a patchwork of fabric pieces. It looks country and creative. It could be used as a gift or a storage box for fabrics.

54

How to Organize Your Closet

Anyone who wants to follow me
must put aside his own desires and
conveniences . . . every day and keep
close to me!
—*Luke 9:23*

*I*S YOUR closet a disaster that gives you the feeling of stress and confusion? Take heart, here's a sensible, easy way to clean it out and put every inch of space to good use. A well-put-together closet makes you more organized and your life just a little bit easier.

Cleaning the Closet

Step 1: Sort clothes into three piles. Hold each item up and ask yourself three questions. Be honest and take time to evaluate. 1) "Do I love it and wear it?" 2) "Do I feel good in it?" You seldom wear clothes you don't feel good in. You hang on to them because you think you are throwing money away if you get rid of them, or because they remind you of the past or because you *may* wear them in the future. Everyone does this. 3) "Am I willing to recycle this?" These are clothes you never wear.

Step 2: Remove the recycle pile. Here are three ways to do this: 1) take the clothes to a used clothing store and earn some extra money, 2) give the clothes to a charity, thrift store, Salvation Army, etc.

(getting a receipt will give you a tax deduction), 3) give the clothes to friends or needy families.

Step 3: Create an ambivalence center. Put the clothes you can't decide about out of the way in storage boxes in an attic, basement, garage, or storage closet. You may decide later to recycle these clothes after all, but for now it may be too emotional.

Step 4: You have now only the "I love to wear" pile to deal with. But why put your clothes back in the same old closet? It may be part of the reason your wardrobe seems to get so disorganized. Let's think about it.

The average closet consists of one long pole beneath one long shelf. The old-fashioned single-pole system wastes usable space. Far more efficient is a system with at least three poles and several shelves. By placing poles at different heights, you increase the number of items you can hang in a given area. In a his-and-her's closet, this technique can quadruple space (see illustrations on the following pages). By discarding the one pole you free space for more shelves. Use these shelves for foldable clothes (enough shelves can eliminate your need for a dresser). By keeping shoes off the floor, you'll eliminate jumbled dusty shoes. Hats and purses go on shelves to make your closet workable and pleasant.

You may want to add a light if there is none. If you have the option, avoid sliding doors. It's best to be able to see all your clothes at once. The floor may need a new look. Try inexpensive self-stick vinyl tiles or carpet remnants. Pretty up your closet with wallpaper, wallpaper borders, paint, posters, or eyelet lace glued on the edge of your shelves. Your new closet will save you both time and money. You'll know exactly where to find things and better yet where to put them back. It will be easier to mix and match outfits when you know what you have and can see everything clearly. You'll be able to expand your wardrobe using what you already own. Now you will enjoy your organized closet. Here are some additional tips:

• One of the reasons most closets are a mess is because people forget about closet organizers. Buy them in notions departments, hardware or dime stores, or use your imagination. These ideas will get you started.

• Mugracks. Good for jewelry, scarves, small purses. Hang vertically or horizontally on closet wall or door.

• Shoebags. Not just for shoes! Use for storing scarves, gloves, stockings . . . anything.

• Hanging baskets. A decorative way to store socks and small, light items.

Figure 7

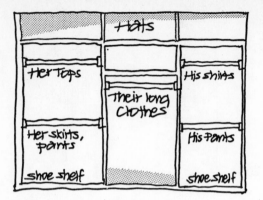

Figure 8

• Kitchen towel racks. Two to four hung on the back of your closet door are great for scarves. Use the thick rounded racks for pants.

• Colorful ceramic hooks. They fit anywhere—for hats, belts, bags, jewelry.

• Pegboards. Hang belts, hats, jewelry—you name it. They are great all-purpose organizers.

• Men's tie and belt racks. Ideal for leotards or lingerie.

• Overhead shoe chests. Ones with dividers and clear plastic zip fronts are an easy way to organize your handbags.

• Shoe boxes. For shoes! Write a description of each pair on the outside. To make them pretty, cover your shoe boxes with wallpaper.

• Plastic bags. *Beware*—do not use for leather bags, furs, boots, shoes, silks, or down vests. These accessories need to breathe.

55

How to Manage Your Mail

There is a time for everything,
and a season for every activity
under heaven.

—*Ecclesiastes 3:1* NIV

*M*ANY OF US can't wait for the mail to come each day. The thought of receiving news from afar is exciting and fresh. At the same time, however, the thought of processing it all can be depressing. Making decisions about what to throw away, what to save, where to put the mail for hubby to read if and when he gets around to it . . . and then, again, what to throw away!

I've discovered three easy steps that have helped me manage my mountains of mail. I hope they work for you too!

1. Designate one area where you open and process all your mail. It could be a desk, a table by a chair, or the kitchen counter. If you use the kitchen counter, however, be careful not to use it as a catchall. One woman told me she put her mail on top of her refrigerator, but it piled up so high it took her three weeks to go through it.

2. Don't let it pile up! Set a time each day when you process your mail. If you can't get to it when you receive your mail, then plan a time when you can. Do it daily.

3. Make decisions. Don't put it down; put it away, and don't be a

mail scooter. It's easy to scoot mail and papers from one area to another, one room to the next, or from one pile to another. Sort out your mail into categories:

- *Throwaway mail*—junk mail, advertisements, etc.
- *Mail you need to read*, but don't have time for now.
- *Mail you need to file away,* such as bills, insurance papers, and receipts.
- *Mail you need to ask someone about*—husband, children, etc.
- *Mail that needs a phone call.* Perhaps you have a question or need a clearer explanation than the letter gave. Many times people ask me questions by letter. If the person is relatively close, I will call rather than write. It is quicker and I can get that letter taken care of faster.
- *Mail to be answered.* Personal letters, forms to be filled out and returned, RSVP's for invitations.

All these categories can be labeled on file folders and put into a file box or metal file cabinet. As soon as the mail comes in, simply slip it into its proper place. Then when your husband comes home you can hand him his folder of mail to read and process.

One woman told me she covered shoeboxes with wallpaper and labeled them, set them in a row on a shelf and processed her mail very quickly. Remember, however, that with file folders or boxes, you still have to beware of pile-ups.

Junk mail is a time waster, so toss it! Don't let yourself say, "I'll probably use this someday," because you very likely will *not*.

On mail that requires other people's input, mark notes or question marks so both of you can discuss it.

There are times when you don't have time to read publications, missionary letters, and magazines. I slip them into a file folder and take the folder along with me in the car. When I have to wait in the doctor's office, for children, or even in a long line, I use that time to catch up on my mail reading. I make notes on it, and then process it according to its category.

Address changes should be made immediately upon receipt, making sure that you dispose of the old address. Also, an RSVP should be answered as soon as you know your plans. This is a common courtesy to your host or hostess; he or she will appreciate your promptness. If you can't give a yes/no answer, then let that be known also.

Mark dates on your calendar as soon as the invitations arrive. Also write down appointments, birthdays, and other significant days. With our busy, busy lives, we can't always depend upon our memories.

56

What to Do with Those Piles of Papers

A wise man thinks ahead; a fool
doesn't, and even brags about it!
—Proverbs 13:16

*E*VERY DAY we make decisions about paper—from personal mail to children's papers, newspapers to magazines to Sunday School papers. We must sort through mountains of paper each week, accumulated from day to day, week to week, and month to month. Some of us find ourselves buried in years of collected, often-forgotten papers.

One woman who attended my seminar shared that she finally had to hire a person to help her organize her papers. A former school teacher, she had acquired volumes of miscellaneous papers.

She and her helper worked three hours a day, five days a week, for three months during summer vacation just organizing paper; a total of 180 hours each!

A lot of time and expense can be avoided if paper is dealt with when it arrives. Rather than stacking it on counters, appliance tops, tables, dressers, or even on the floor until it takes up nearly every empty space in our homes, we need to file and/or dispose of paper as soon as it is received.

Another lady confessed that she couldn't use her dining room table without a major paper transfer before entertaining company. Still another woman shared that her husband threatened, "It's either me or the papers that go." Needless to say, she began a major paper-filing program and quickly got the paper epidemic under control.

Paper disorganization often begins in subtle ways. With only insurance policies, checking account statements, and canceled checks, car registrations, apartment rental agreements, birth certificates, a marriage license, diplomas, and a few other miscellaneous papers, a person often reasons that a full-fledged filing system is not necessary. Thus the file often consists of merely a cardboard shoe-box or metal, fireproof box which can easily be stored away on a closet shelf.

As the years go by, however, there are "his" papers, "her" papers, appliance warranties, and instruction booklets on the television, the toaster, and the lawn mower (along with other gadgets too numerous to mention). The result is paper chaos.

Don't despair. Help is on the way. Here are six simple steps to effective paper-management.

1. *Schedule set times* for sorting through papers.
2. *Collect materials* you will need to help you get organized.
   - Metal file cabinet or file boxes.
   - Plastic trash bags.
   - File folders. (I prefer bright colored folders, but plain manila will do.)
   - Black felt marking pen.
3. *Begin.*
   - Start with whatever room annoys you the most. Work your way through every pile of paper; go through drawers and closets. Then move on to rooms where other papers have accumulated. Continue at set times until your project is completed.
4. *Throw away.*
   - Be determined. Make decisions. Throw away the clutter.
   - Perhaps you have lots of articles, recipes, or children's school papers and artwork which you have been saving for that special "someday." In each category, choose five pieces to keep and get rid of the rest! Try not to be too sentimental.
   - Keep the saving of papers to a minimum. Put the throwaway papers into bags and carry them out to the trash. Don't wait. It's a good feeling!
   - Don't get bogged down rereading old letters, recipes, articles, etc. It's easy to spend too much time reminiscing and get sidetracked from your purpose of streamlining your paper-filing system.

• Keep legal papers a minimum of seven years.

• If you have trouble determining what to throw away, ask a friend to help you make some of those decisions. Friends tend to be more objective and you can return the favor when they discover how "organized" you are.

5. *File.*

• Keep your filing system as simple as possible. If it is too detailed and complex, you may be easily discouraged.

• Categorize the papers you want to save (i.e., magazine articles, Bible study notes/outlines, family information, IRS papers, bank statements/ canceled checks, charge accounts, utilities, taxes, house, and investments).

• Label the file folders with a felt pen.

• Within each category, mark a folder or envelope for each separate account. For example, in the utilities, water, gasoline, and telephone. In the insurance folder, it is helpful to designate separate envelopes for life, health, car and house insurance.

• Label a folder for each member of the family. These can be used for keeping health records, report cards, notes, drawings, awards, and other special remembrances.

• Other suggestions for categories: vacation possibilities, Christmas card lists, home improvement ideas, warranties, instruction booklets, photos/negatives, and car/home repair receipts.

• File papers in appropriate folders. *Do it at the time they are received and/or paid.* (Especially take care to file away your check stubs, paid receipts, and other budget records on the day you receive your paycheck.)

• Place files in cabinet or boxes and store.

6. *Store.*

• Store files (cabinets or boxes) in a closet, garage, attic, or some other area that is out of sight, yet easily accessible.

• Be sure to label the file boxes. (I use a 3 x 5 card stapled on the end of the box with the contents written on the card. Then if I empty the box at a later date, I can easily tear off the card and replace it with another card, or use the box for other items.)

Remember, you don't need to buy a home computer to help you get organized. You do, however, need to start right where you are . . . tackling your own mountains of paper by filing and storing the information you want, and disposing of the clutter that depresses and discourages you.

57

Babysitting Survival Guide

*Don't copy the behavior and
customs of this world, but be a new
and different person with a fresh
newness in all you do and think.*
—*Romans 12:2*

*S*IXTEEN-YEAR OLD Lynn arrives at
the Merrihew home, eager to take care of
Craig and Jenny's three adorable children. Craig, Jenny, and Lynn
chat briefly, and then Craig and Jenny go out the door, delighted to
have their first date alone in six weeks.

About 45 minutes later, two-year old Christine is still crying and
screaming, "Mommy!" Lynn remembers that Craig and Jenny were
going to be at three different places during the evening, but she can't
remember what time they were to be where. She's not even sure if
she should call them.

Meanwhile Craig and Jenny keep remembering things they
wished they had told Lynn. Their intimate conversation is interrupted by an ongoing debate as to whether to call home.

Whether your babysitter is 16 or 66, there are certain steps you
can take to insure a smoother and more enjoyable evening for sitter
and parents alike. I call these "survival hints."

For Mom and Dad

• Agree on an hourly fee with your sitter when you make the babysitting arrangement.

• Ask a first-time sitter to arrive early so you and your children can get acquainted with the sitter. This gives your sitter the chance to become familiar with your home before you leave.

• Explain your home rules about snacking, visitors, television, and the stereo.

• Tell the sitter what time each child is to go to bed and whether your child has any special needs, such as a favorite toy, blanket, or story.

• Show the sitter, if necessary, procedures for feeding, warming a bottle, and changing a diaper.

• Write down the instructions as to time and dosage for any medications your child may be taking. Leave these next to the bottle with a measuring spoon or dropper nearby.

• Let your sitter know at the time of hiring whether he or she will be expected to prepare and serve a meal.

• Make special arrangements at the time you hire your sitter if you want him or her to do any housework. Most parents pay extra for that service.

• Place a flashlight in a handy place in case of power failure.

• Leave a pad and pen by the phone for phone messages and notes of the evening's events.

• Call home periodically if the sitter will not be able to reach you easily.

• Phone your sitter if you will be arriving home later than you had planned. Let him or her know when you expect to arrive.

• Pay your sitter the previously agreed-upon fee when you return home, unless you have worked out another payment arrangement ahead of time. Be aware that checks are sometimes hard for teenagers to cash. Some parents pay extra for hours after midnight. (If you must cancel a sitter at the last minute, it is courteous to pay the sitter for part of the time he or she was planning on working for you.)

For the Babysitter

• Be sure you understand what is expected of you. Don't count on your memory; write instructions down if the list gets too long.

• Be sure you know where parents or other adults such as grandparents or aunts and uncles can be reached at all times.

• Request that the children be present when parents give you instructions so you all understand the rules.

• Don't open the doors for strangers. (Any deliveries can be left outside or delivered later when the parents are home.)

• Keep all outside doors locked at all times.

• Don't tell telephone callers that parents are not at home. Take a message if possible, and tell the caller that they will return the call when they are able to come to the phone.

• Keep your own phone calls brief.

• Clean up your own mess. Any extra effort you make will encourage the parents to call you again.

• Don't snoop in closets or drawers. Even though you are working in the home, you are still a guest.

• Try to stay alert and awake unless it is a long, late evening.

• Inform the parents of any illness or accident, however minor, or any item broken while they were gone. Accidents do happen, and most parents allow for this.

• Tell parents as soon as possible if you have to cancel.

• Take a first-aid course at your local YWCA, Red Cross, or Community Service Department. Some cities have regular classes designed for babysitters. If not, buy a first-aid handbook.

58

Garage Sale Organization

Fear not, for I am with you. Do not
be dismayed. I am your God. I will
strengthen you; I will help you; I
will uphold you.

—*Isaiah 41:10*

*A*S SUMMER comes to an end and you need something to keep your restless children busy, why not plan a garage sale? Tell them that they can keep the money from the sale of their items, and you'll be surprised at how quickly they get motivated to clean their rooms and get rid of clutter.

Not only will a garage sale tidy up your home, it can also be quite profitable. Our children often use their money to buy back-to-school supplies and new clothes. Another good idea is to give the money to a church project or a missionary family. After you help your children decide how they want to use the money they make, put on your grubbies, roll up your sleeves, and start planning.

Set your date. The first step is to set your garage sale date. It is best to plan a one-day sale, either on a Friday or Saturday. Once that is set, call the newspaper or community shopper handout and place an advertisement.

Your ad should be short, to the point, and should *not* include your phone number. You don't need to answer a lot of phone calls and silly questions. Here is a sample ad:

Garage Sale—Saturday, Sept. 6, 9 A.M. to 5 P.M.
Bookcase—toys—antiques—appliances—clothing—
bike—tools and lots of goodies. 6256 Windemere Way,
Chicago at Ransom Road.

Make your signs. Use heavy cardboard or brightly colored poster board and bold felt pens in contrasting colors. Keep it simple. Merely write: "GARAGE SALE," your house address, and street name. Most people don't need too much prompting to drive by a garage sale. My car goes on automatic when it sees a garage sale sign, and stops dead-center in front of the house!

When placing your signs, make sure they are in a prominent location. Use your own stakes. Do not put them on top of a street sign or speed-limit sign. Always go back and remove your signs the day after your sale.

Make your decisions. Now comes the cleaning out and decision-making process. Spend time with each child going over the items they begin to pull out of their rooms. They sometimes get so excited that they want to sell their bed, favorite teddy bear, and even the dog or cat.

You'll have to watch yourself too. I got so excited at one of our garage sales that I sold our refrigerator! People were coming and buying so fast that I got all caught up in it. I didn't like our refrigerator anyway and thought a new one would be great. Besides, it looked like we were selling plenty and bringing in a lot of money. A couple asked me what else I had for sale and I said, "How about the refrigerator?" They bought it.

I was thrilled—until my husband, Bob, came home. I learned a good lesson: Keep your cool and don't lose your head!

Organize. Display items in categories. For example, put all the toys in one place, and glassware and kitchen utensils in another. Place breakable items on tables if possible.

Have an extension cord available from your garden or house outlet so people can check electrical appliances such as a popcorn popper, iron, razor, or clock. If the item does not work, tell the truth. Your interested customer may still buy it. Many garage shoppers are handymen who can fix anything or can use the parts from a nonworking item.

Hospitality gives a garage sale an added touch. Try serving fresh coffee, tea, or iced tea.

Set your price. Pricing takes a lot of time and thought. As a general rule, keep your prices down. Never mark your price directly on the article. If your husband's shirt doesn't sell, he may go to the office one day with $1.50 inked on his cuff or pocket. It is best to use stick-on labels, round stickers, or masking tape.

If individual family members are going to keep the money from the sale of particular items, be sure to mark them with appropriate initials or a color code (Linda has the blue label, Tom has the green).

I always price everything in increments of 50 cents—$1.50, $2.50, etc. That way you have some bargaining power. People love bargains.

It's a good idea to have separate boxes containing items priced at five cents, ten cents, and 25 cents. This will save you from having to mark each item separately. Children love these boxes because then they can shop while mom and dad look around. You can even have a box marked "FREE."

Have one person, preferably an adult, be the cashier. All purchases must go through that person. Take a large sheet of poster board and list each person who is selling at your sale. As each item is sold, take off the price sticker and place it under his or her name or write the price in the appropriate column. At the end of the day, simply add up each column. It's best to accept only cash from your customer.

Make time count. On the day of the sale, get up early and commit the day to the sale. Eat a good breakfast; you'll need a clear mind for bargain decisions. Since people interested in antiques and valuable items will come by early, it is best to have everything set up the day before. Then all you have to do on the morning of the sale is to move your tables of items outside on the walkway, patio, or driveway.

Pack lunches the night before for you and your children. You won't have time to make lunch with people in your yard all day. Aim toward having a calm, loving spirit, and keep the family involved and available to help. Remember, this is a family project.

By the end of the day, you'll be ready for a hot bath and a chance to relax. Pop some popcorn, sit down with your family, and enjoy discussing the day's activities and the way you'll use your profits.

59

You're Moving... Again?

What is faith? It is the confident
assurance that something we want
is going to happen.
—*Hebrews 11:1*

I HAVE A friend whose husband serves
in the U.S. Army. Every time she
finally finishes unpacking the last box and begins to feel somewhat
acclimated to her new surroundings, her husband comes home from
work and says, "Well, it's time to pack up, we're moving next
month." In the past 11 years they've moved 11 times.

To most people, the thought of moving does not exactly bring
cheers or happy memories. It can, however, be an easy and smooth
process if preplanned and organized.

Before you even begin to organize your move, however, two
questions need to be answered clearly: 1) How long do you have to
plan your move—one week, one month, or six months? 2) How are
you going to move—a "do it yourself" move, a moving company, or
a combination of both?

Once you know when and how you are moving, you are ready to
begin.

Step 1: Household Check off List

There are so many details to remember before moving time, and often important things are forgotten until it's too late. Here is a checklist of the essential details that must be taken care of:

Transfer of Records
- School records
- Auto registration and driver's license
- Bank—savings and checking accounts
- Medical records from doctors and dentists
- Eyeglass prescription
- Pet immunization records
- Legal documents
- Church and other organizations
- Insurance

Services to Be Discontinued
- Telephone company
- Electric, gas, and water company
- Layaway purchases
- Cleaners—don't move without picking up all your clothes
- Fuel company
- Milk delivery
- Newspaper delivery
- Cable television
- Pest control
- Water softener or bottled water
- Garbage service
- Diaper service

Change of Address
- Local post office
- Magazines
- Friends and relatives
- Insurance company
- Creditors and charge accounts
- Lawyer
- Church

Step 2: Getting Ready

- Reserve a moving company if needed.
- Prepare to pack by enlisting some volunteers. Neighbors or friends from church are likely candidates and usually very willing to help.

• Collect boxes from local supermarkets and drugstores. Be sure to go to stores early in the day before the boxes are flattened and thrown out. Some moving companies will loan you boxes such as wardrobe boxes.

• Buy felt marking pens to color-code your boxes. (More details on how to do this later.)

• Prepare a work area such as a card table that can be used for wrapping and packing your goods.

• Clean and air the refrigerator and kitchen range.

• Be sure that gas appliances are properly disconnected.

• Make a list of items that need special care when being packed, such as your antique lamp or china cup-and-saucer collection.

• Discard flammable materials—empty gas tanks on mowers and chain saw.

• Be sure to leave space open in your driveway or on the street for your truck, trailer, or moving van.

• Keep handy a small box of tools to dismantle furniture with a bucket, rags, and cleaning products to clean your home after it is empty.

Step 3: Packing

Packing your goods properly is the most important part of your move. A little care on your part can assure that none of your things will be damaged.

Use good, sturdy boxes that you can depend on for protection, and be generous in padding your belongings with paper. Packing paper can be purchased at low cost at your local newspaper plant. This unprinted paper is super for wrapping dishes and glassware.

• Begin packing boxes, if possible, two weeks ahead of moving day.

• Either use colored pens or a number system and mark each box to identify its contents and the room where it is to go. For example: yellow—kitchen; green—garden and garage; blue—Brad's bedroom.

Or number your boxes 1, 2, 3, etc. Then make out 3 x 5 cards and number them Box 1, Box 2, etc. List on each card what is in each box and to which room it belongs. Put your 3 x 5 cards in a small box. On moving day, as each numbered box is carried into the house, direct it to the appropriate room.

Because you know by your numbered cards what is in each box without opening it, you can unpack the priority boxes first. This is also a great method for organizing the goods you plan to store in your basement or attic.

• Moving is a good time to weed out things you need to get rid of. Although some items should just be thrown out, other things such as old clothing can be given to churches, orphanages, or the Salvation Army.

Other ways to get rid of excess items are to run an ad in your local paper, or hold a garage sale.

Remember, when you give away items to nonprofit groups, you can use the net value as a deduction from your income tax. Be sure to get a signed receipt.

• Don't pack fragile and heavy items in the same box.

• Use smaller boxes for heavier items and larger boxes for light-weight, bulky items.

• Fill each box completely and compactly. Don't overfill or under-fill.

• When packing glass dishes, put a paper plate between each plate as a protector. Stack plates on end (not flat). They seem to take the pressure better when packed that way.

• Popcorn is another good packing agent for china cups and crystal glasses. Fill the cups and glasses with popcorn and wrap them in your unprinted paper. Foam padding also works well to protect your breakables.

• To protect your mirrors and paintings, cut cardboard to fit around them, bind them with tape and label them "FRAGILE."

• When packing your tables, if possible remove their legs and pack them on edge. If this is not possible, load tables with their surface down and legs up. Take care to protect the finish with blankets or other padding.

Furniture pads can be wrapped around items and tied together or sewn together temporarily with heavy thread.

• Seal boxes with packing tape, or put the boxes into trash bags and then tape.

• Move your dresser drawers with the clothes inside.

• Be sure bathroom items, medicines, and cleaning agents are packed and sealed immediately so small children cannot get to them.

Loading Your Van, Truck, or Trailer

• Park next to the widest door of your home and leave enough room to extend a ramp if necessary.

• Load your vehicle one quarter at a time, using all the space from floor to ceiling. Try to load weight evenly from side to side to prevent it from shifting.

• Put heaviest items in front.

• Tie off each quarter with rope. This will keep your goods from banging up against each other and getting damaged.

• Use a dolly for the heavy items. (These can be rented from rental equipment or moving companies.) CAUTION: When lifting heavy objects, bend your knees and use your leg muscles. Keep your back as straight as possible.

• Fit bicycles and other odd-shaped items along the walls of the truck or on top of stacked items.

Finish cleaning up your house, lock your door, and you're on your way!

Corralling
the Chaos

*She watches carefully all that goes
on throughout her household, and is
never lazy.*

—Proverbs 31:27

ONE SUNDAY after church service my husband, Bob, and I were visiting with some friends. When one woman asked me about my "More Hours In My Day" ministry, I told her about some of the recent seminars I had conducted around the country.

All of a sudden, a man who was listening to our conversation grabbed my arm. "Emilie, our family lives in a cesspool," he complained. Thankfully, his wife was not within earshot.

"My wife doesn't work. We have three children; two of them are in school. Yet she says she doesn't have time to clean the house."

Do you think this is an isolated case? It isn't. In today's hectic society, men and women are so busy that often there is no time left to plan and execute the daily routines of life.

For many people, life is lived in a constant panic, trying to stay on top of the house, family, and career. With more women in the work force, there has never been a greater need for basic organizational skills in our homes.

Establishing the Target

If you don't have a goal for organizing your home and life, you can never know if you have hit or missed the target. Much time is wasted because we don't know where we're going.

Early in our marriage Bob and I felt it was important to set goals. We dreamed of the type of home and family we wanted. We realized that in order to achieve those dreams we needed a plan. That plan became the "Barnes' Family Life Goals."

We talked often of those goals, and periodically we adjusted them as our lives changed. The biggest change came as we began to mature in our Christian faith. That's when our goals became more Christ-centered.

Goal-setting doesn't just happen. You must take time to think long-range in order to effectively plan for the next few years. And your goals must be important enough to work at making them happen.

Bob and I have set ten-year goals and then we've broken those down into smaller goals. Where do we want to be in five years if we're to fulfill our ten-year goals? What about three years? One year? Six months? Three months? One month? Today?

See the progression? How can we plan today if we don't know where we're headed? Sure, we can fill our time with activities; that's easy. But by goal-setting, everything we do is directed toward a purpose that we've set.

Priorities—What Comes First?

Jean had set her goals and organized her days according to those goals. But she never was able to complete her daily TO DO list.

I asked Jean to show me a typical list of her day's priorities. With 16 activities written on her list, Jean realized she could not possibly do every one of them. She needed to divide these options into three categories:

Yes: I will do this.

Maybe: I will do this if there is time.

No: I will not attempt this today.

Notice the last option? You must learn to say "NO!" Too many women assume that their only options are "yes" and "maybe." If we can't say no to some things, we become overcommitted and wind up carrying heavy loads of guilt because of unfulfilled commitments.

Making Decisions Using Priorities

Just how does a Christian proceed with decisions when the answers are not obvious?

Priority 1: GOD

According to Matthew 6:33, our first priority is to seek and know God. This is a lifelong pursuit. When God has first place in our lives, deciding among the other alternatives is easier.

When I feel hassled or hurried, it's often because this priority is out of order. Usually I need to adjust my schedule in order to spend time with God. When I allow Him to fill my heart, I can relax and have a clearer perspective on the rest of my activities.

Priority 2: FAMILY

In Proverbs 31 we read about the woman who "watches carefully all that goes on throughout her household, and is never lazy. Her children stand and bless her; so does her husband" (verses 27,28).

How does a woman receive such praise from her family? The answer is by providing a home setting full of warmth, love, and respect.

Priority 3: CHURCH-RELATED ACTIVITIES

Hebrews 10:25 tells us to be involved in our church, but that is not at the expense of the first two priorities.

Priority 4: ALL OTHER AREAS

This includes job, exercise, classes, clubs, and other activities. Some people are amazed that there is time for any of these items. But there is.

God wants you to live a balanced life, and that means you need time for work and time for recreation—time to cut some flowers, drink a cup of tea, or go shopping with a friend. These activities can revitalize you for the responsibilities of home and church.

With these priorities in mind, Jean attacked her list of activities, beginning with the junk mail. "I think I'll just toss the whole pile," she said. By eliminating three more activities and putting four in the "maybe" category, Jean was immediately more relaxed.

I encouraged her to cross off the "yes" activities as she completed each one to give herself the satisfaction of seeing the list shrink during the day. If time permitted, she could do the "maybe" activities, but if she didn't, some of them might become "yes" activities on another day.

Of course, not all decisions can be made swiftly—some require more time and consideration. I've made Paul Little's five-point outline from his booklet *Affirming the Will of God* my criteria when I have trouble establishing my priorities:

1. Pray with an attitude of obedience to the Lord. God's promise to us is, "I will instruct you and teach you in the way you should go; I will counsel you and watch over you" (Psalm 32:8 NIV).

2. What does the Bible say that might guide me in making the decision? "Be diligent to present yourself approved to God as a workman . . . handling accurately the word of truth" (2 Timothy 2:15 NASB).

3. Obtain information from competent sources in order to gain all the pertinent facts. "A wise man's heart directs him toward the right" (Ecclesiastes 10:2 NASB).

4. Obtain advice from people knowledgeable about the issue. It's best if our counselors are fellow Christians who can pray with and for us. "Iron sharpens iron, so one man sharpens another" (Proverbs 27:17 NASB).

5. Make the decision without second-guessing God. "He who trusts in the Lord will prosper" (Proverbs 28:25 NASB).

The purpose of establishing priorities is to avoid becoming over-extended. If you know you are always doing the most important activities first, you can relax even when you cannot complete everything on your TO DO list.

Family Conference Time

Probably the number-one question women ask me when I give a seminar is "How do I get my husband and children involved?" That's a tough question to answer because each family is different.

One mistake many women make is that they assume every family member understands his or her role. They never discuss their expectations with their husband or children. With many mothers working, it is often necessary for other family members to assume some of the responsibilities that are traditionally the woman's. The family needs to understand the concept of *teamwork*.

Mom is not the only player in the family—everyone plays a valuable part. So I first recommend that moms stop carrying the whole team. That only leads to tired, burned-out, frustrated women.

It did not take the Barnes family long to realize that we need a regular time to discuss important topics. One of our long-range goals was to raise independent and responsible children, and Bob and I felt that one way to achieve this goal was to allow our children to be part of the decision-making process.

Yet how could we set aside more time when everyone was already busy with many activities? Our solution also resolved another chronic problem in our home.

Probably the most hectic time for our family was Sunday morning before church. Mom and dad often had a few cross words because we were late. By the time we drove into the church parking lot, we were rarely in a mood for worship.

In order to solve our two problems—stressful Sundays and the need for family meetings—we decided to start going out for breakfast on Sunday mornings before church. Overnight we saw improvement.

Eating breakfast out eliminated the problem of food preparation and cleanup, and it gave us time to discuss various aspects of our family life. We established Sunday breakfasts as part of our regular monthly budget, and all of us looked forward to this time together.

Our family activities and conference times played a valuable part in establishing harmony, respect, and pride within our family. Not every meeting and activity was a success, but we usually gained greater respect for one another.

Family Work Planner

One idea that helped our family better distribute the housework was to establish a "Daily Work Planner." We would write the weekly chores on separate slips of paper, place them in a basket, and every Saturday each of us drew one or more slips to learn our duties for the upcoming week.

As each assignment was drawn, it was recorded on the Daily Work Planner, which was posted in a conspicuous place. Each family member was responsible to complete his assignment. Mom and dad also drew their chores from the basket—this was a team effort.

If your children range widely in their ages, you may want to use two baskets—one for smaller children and one for the rest of the family. In this way, the younger children do not draw jobs that are too difficult for them.

It is also important that mom and dad inspect the work to make sure chores are being done properly. Occasionally, give a special reward for a job well done.

Please note that I am not suggesting that children assume the load in maintaining a house. As parents you must allow your children to participate in their own activities. They need time to get involved in sports, music, homework, and other school and church activities.

You also need to recognize your priorities in relating to your mate. When my children were still at home, I often remembered the saying, "You were a wife to your husband before you were a mother to your children." Our children will grow up and leave home (hopefully). However, we will still have our mate after the nest is empty.

A couple needs to spend quality time with each other without the children. You must not use the excuse that you can't afford to do it. You can't afford *not* to. Bob and I plan times together and reserve those days on our calendar just as we would any other appointment. We protect those times and don't cancel them unless there is an emergency.

For single parents who are raising children alone, the pressures are even more intense, especially when the children are young. I believe the family conference time and division of responsibilities can help relieve some of the pressure. However, sometimes as a parent—whether married, single, or widowed—you may have to leave some things unfinished rather than continue to tax your spirit.

There are no rules on how a home should be run; each family needs to set its own standards. My family enjoys working together as we set joint goals, but it is a process that takes time.

In his first letter, the apostle Peter wrote that wives could influence their husbands: "Even if any of them are disobedient to the word, they may be won without a word by the behavior of their wives" (1 Peter 3:1 NASB).

Even though the context of this verse deals with salvation, Peter provides an excellent principle. In our society, the mother sets the tone for the family and home. Many times, dad and junior are not as excited about the home as mom is. If you are aware of this truth, you will be disappointed less often because you will not have as many expectations.

We need to remind ourselves that it is not our role to change our husband and children. God will do that in His time. We must be faithful to the Scriptures and love our family even when they may not return that love.

It is important to realize that there are many areas of stress that you can relieve. I have attempted to give some practical helps in many of those areas. Implementing these organizational techniques can help you enjoy more hours in your day and experience more joy in your home.

Keeping Track of Loaned and Borrowed Items

To err is human, to forgive, divine.

 $\mathscr{F}$ OR MANY YEARS I loaned items to my friends thinking I would surely remember who had my turkey platter, Tupperware bowls, picnic basket, and the children's sleeping bags. You know what? I forgot after a short period of time. There was no way I could remember, no matter how hard I tried.

It's even more embarrassing to find you have items that don't belong to you and you can't remember who you borrowed them from.

We once had some brick masonry work done on our home and in talking with our contractor he said he had loaned over $500.00 worth of tools to friends but couldn't remember who the friends were. I showed him the form I use and he thought it would be of real value to him (see page 229, Figure 9).

This form will fit very nicely into your 8½ x 5½ organizer notebook for ease in keeping track of all your records.

Remember to form new habits you must be consistent in using your new organization tools.

ITEMS LOANED/BORROWED

Month/Year January – February 1991

Date	Item	Who	Returned
1/3	Cake plate	Church	✓
1/4	Screwdriver	Charlie	✓
1/7	Circular saw	Jimmy	✓
1/15	Plastic cups (10)	Brownies	✓
1/22	Lawn mower	George	✓
1/27	Card table	Christine	✓
1/29	Diving mask	Youth group	✓
2/4	Tent	Scout troop	✓
2/5	Posthole digger	Mr. Brown	✓
2/9	Snow White video	daughter	✓
2/12	Pewter pitcher	Georgia	✓

Figure 9

One other reminder is to personally identify items you loan with your name and telephone number. This technique will also help get back those missing items.

Make them loaned, not lost!

Keeping Track of Those On-Order Products

A good wife watches for bargains.
—*Proverbs 31:18*

*H*AVE YOU forgotten which manufacturer's rebate coupons you have sent in for a refund, or that blouse you have on order from your favorite catalogue? Well, now you can spend a few minutes recording those "on-order" items that need to be tracked until they have been received (see page 233, Figure 10). I even use this form to track refunds from my Visa card and the utility companies.

Add this form to your organizer notebook along with an index tab for easy location and you can keep an easy record.

There are two rules to remember when using an organizer to help you stay on track:

• You must write it down.
• You must read it.

It takes 21 days to form a new habit, so continue to write down what's on order. There are many good commercially manufactured organizer notebooks, for which you can pay anywhere from $40.00 to $250.00. Or you can be industrious and make your own organizer. All you need is:

- one 8¹/₂ x 5¹/₂ three-ring binder
- ten 8¹/₂ x 5¹/₂ index tabs for labeling and dividing your paper by sections
- fifty 8¹/₂ x 5¹/₂ lined paper
- one 8¹/₂ x 5¹/₂ month-at-a-glance calendar on two pages
- thirty 8¹/₂ x 5¹/₂ daily calendar pages to help you through each day

On Order

Date Ordered	Item	Company	Date Due	Received
1/6	white blouse	Lands End	1/20	✓
1/6	red socks	"	1/20	✓
1/6	plaid slacks	"	1/20	BO
2/3	crib sheets	J.C. Penny	2/17	✓
2/3	crib mattress	"	2/17	✓
2/15	Patio lights $1.00 rebate	Malibu Lights		
2/18	Gas rebate $12.00	Southern CA Gas Co.	3/1	✓
2/22	Credit $17.00	Bank Visa	3/10	✓
2/27	Coupon rebate $1.50	Campbell Soup		
3/2	T-shirts	Sears	3/14	
3/2	white socks	"	3/14	
3/2	Levis	"	3/14	

Figure 10

Setting Up
a Desk
and Work Area

The effective prayer of a righteous
man can accomplish much.
—*James 5:16* NASB

*A*S I BEGAN to get my home in order
and to eliminate all the clutter I soon
realized that I didn't have an area to handle all the mail and paper that
came into our home. We have had several mottos to help us focus in
on our home organization.

One was **"Don't put it down, put it away."** Much of our clutter
was little piles of materials that needed to be put away, but we just
temporarily put it down until we could put it where it belonged. At
the end of the day we had piles sitting all around the home. Now we
take the material back to where we found it. Amazing how the piles
have disappeared.

Another motto was **"Don't pile it, file it."** Somewhere in the
corner of the home we had piles of paper that were in no organized
fashion. In our new program we have taken manila folders and given
them one-word headings such as: insurance, car, home, foods, patio,
children, utilities, taxes. Now we file, not pile our papers.

During all this change in our home, we still had no central desk or
work area. Yet we had recognized that we needed one in order to

function properly and with maximum efficiency.

Paper-handling depends upon a good physical setting with a practical location furnished with a comfortable working surface and a good inventory of supplies. Ideally, this office will become a permanent fixture where the business life of your home is done. It should be accessible, with supplies and files, and located where other household operations do not interfere. However, if your desk/work area can't be this ideal, don't let this stop you from getting started. Your work area might have to be portable, but that's okay. The important thing is to *just get started*.

Since a desk or work area is so basic to a well-functioning lifestyle, we will give you some practical steps in setting up this area in your home.

Choosing the Location

Where your office will be should depend upon how long you plan to spend in your office daily. If you operate a business out of your home you will need to use different criteria in selecting that special site, giving preference to the needs of the business over those of the person who needs a place to open mail, answer mail, pay bills, and file papers. In either case, you want to choose a location that agrees with your spirit. If after a short while you find you aren't using your new space, but rather find yourself working in the room with a big window, you may have initially selected the wrong location. Make sure the location meets your needs. In order to help you choose that ideal setting, you might ask yourself these questions:

• Do you need to be in a place where it's quiet, or is it better for you to be near people?

• Do big windows distract you, or do you like being near windows?

• Do you prefer a sunny room or a shaded one?

• Do you prefer to work in the morning or in the afternoon?

These last two questions are related because different rooms receive varying amounts of light at different times of the day.

The answer to these questions helps narrow your alternatives. Walk around your home to see which areas meet the answers to your four questions. After selecting at least two locations, you might ask yourself another set of questions:

• Are there enough electrical outlets and telephone jacks?

• Is there enough space for a desk?

• Is this location out of the way of other household functions? If not, can the activities be shifted so they won't interfere with your office hours?

• Is the area structurally sound?

Again, add the answers to these questions to your previously selected alternatives and narrow your choices to a final selection. Do you feel good about this selection? Live with it a few days before making a final decision. Walk to and through it several times to make sure it feels good. Sit down in the area and read a magazine or book. If it still feels good, then you will probably like your choice.

Don't begin tearing out walls, adding electrical outlets, moving phone jacks, or building bookcases until you are sure it's the right location.

Selection of Desk, Equipment, and Supplies

After you have selected the location for your office, you need to take a sheet of paper and make a diagram of the floor plan with the dimensions listed. You will use this information when you want to make or select furniture for your new work area.

The Desk

In actuality, all one really needs is a writing surface of some type. In some cases a piece of plywood is all you may have or need. Look around. You may already have around your home a suitable desk or table which would fit into the dimensions of the work area.

If you find a table, it should be sturdy, high enough to write comfortably, and large enough to hold various implements on its surface.

If you can't find a desk or table in your home, buy a desk. It is an investment you won't regret. Check your local classified ads to find a good bargain. Another good place to look is in the yellow pages of your phone book under "Office Furniture—Used." You need not pay full price, and many times these stores will deliver to your home free or with a minimum charge.

You should have no trouble finding a desk which has the practical characteristics of office models, but is still attractive in your home. Here are a few specifications to keep in mind.

1. *Writing surface:* Your desk should be sturdy and comfortable to use, with a surface that doesn't wobble.

2. *Place for supplies:* Your desk should have at least one large drawer in which paper and envelopes can be kept in folders. If you find a desk with large drawers on each side, so much the better. There needs to be a shallow drawer with compartments for paper clips, rubber bands, and other supplies. Or you can purchase small trays with dividers that can store these small items at your local stationery store.

3. *Files and records:* A home office seldom has need for more than one file drawer, or sometimes two. If your desk has at least one drawer big enough to contain letter-size file folders (legal-size accommodation is preferable), all your files will probably fit. If you can't purchase a file cabinet at this time, use Perfect boxes until you are able to purchase a file cabinet. Watch your newspaper for stationery "sale" offerings.

4. *Typing platform:* If you have a typewriter or a personal computer and plan to use it in your work area, try to get a desk with a built-in platform for these to rest on. If you have enough room in your office you might want to designate separate areas for these two functions.

If you don't have enough space for a regular stationery desk in your home, look into portable storage to house your stationery and supplies. Go again to your local office supply store and have them recommend products that will service this need. You will still need a file cabinet or its short-term substitute (the Perfect Box) and a sturdy swivel chair just for the office area. The swivel chair permits you to turn from one position to another without getting up.

Other Storage Ideas

• Wall organizers are helpful for pads, pens, calendars, and other supplies.

• Paper, pencils, and supplies can be kept in stackable plastic or vinyl storage cubes kept under the desk.

• Use an extra bookcase shelf for a portable typewriter, a basket of supplies, or some files.

• Decorative objects such as a ceramic mug look attractive holding pencils and pens.

• Use stackable plastic bins that can be added to as your needs expand. Use the small style for stationery and papers, and a larger size (a vegetable bin) for magazines and newspapers.

Supplies

For your shopping convenience I have given you a checklist of supplies that you will need to stock your office. Again, try to purchase these items on sale or at an office supply discount store. Watch your local paper for these sales. Or again, let the yellow pages do the walking for you. Look under "Office Supplies." Many times bulk buying is where you will get your best prices.

___ *Address book or Rolodex.* I personally like both; the address book I take with me when I'm traveling or on business, and a Rolodex is permanently housed on my desk. The Rolodex also has more room for adding other information you might want to use when addressing a particular person/business.

_____ *Appointment calendar.* Ideally the calendar should be small enough to carry around with your notebook, as well as for use at your desk. If you search around you can find a combination notebook and calendar that isn't too bulky to carry around in your briefcase or handbag. The date squares should be large enough to list appointments comfortably. In our *Working Woman's Seminars* we offer an excellent organizer called the *Harper House/Day Runner.* This product does an excellent job meeting this need.

_____ *Bulletin board.* This is a good place to collect notes and reminders to yourself. Attach notes with push pins.

_____ *Business cards.* A must time-saver.

_____ *Carbon paper.* Make a carbon copy of every business letter you write. Your office supply store can help you with this selection. Every year new formats come on the market.

_____ *Desk lamp.* A three-way bulb will give you a choice of light.

_____ *Dictionary and/or electronic spell-checker.*

_____ *File folders.* I use colored "third-cut" folders in which the stick-up tabs are staggered so they don't block my view of other folders. The colors give a more attractive appearance to my file drawer.

_____ *Letter opener.*

_____ *Marking pens.* It is useful to have on hand a few marking pens in different colors. I do a lot of color-coding on my calendar. I also use a yellow highlighter when I want some information to pop out at me for rereading.

_____ *Paper clips.* Regular and large.

_____ *Postcards.* Saves money on your mailing.

_____ *Pencil sharpener.* If you use a lot of pencils, I recommend a desktop electric model.

_____ *Pencils and pens.*

_____ *Postage scale.* A small inexpensive type.

_____ *Rubber bands.* Mixed sizes.

_____ *Rubber stamp and inkpad.* There are all kinds of rubber stamps that you can use in your office. These are much cheaper than printed stationery or labels. If you use a certain one over and over, you might consider having a self-inking stamp made for you. A great time-saver.

____ *Ruler.*

____ *Scissors.*

____ *Scratch paper.* Use lined pads for this. Post-it-Notes are also great.

____ *Scotch tape and dispenser.*

____ *Stamps.* In addition to regular stamps, keep appropriate postage on hand for additional weight and special handling if you have special needs regularly. Postcards will save you money on certain types of correspondence.

____ *Stapler, staples, staple remover.* If you do a lot of stapling you might consider an electric model. Saves time and the palm of your hand.

____ *Stationery and envelopes.* Usually 8½ x 11 plain white paper with matching business-size envelopes is all you need. If you use printed letterhead stationery you will need to get some plain white or matching colored second sheets. I find 9 x 6 and 9 x 12 manila envelopes good for mailing bulk documents, books, or magazines. Sometimes padded envelopes are needed to ship items that need some protection from rough handling in transit.

____ *Telephone.* An extension right at your desk is great. I use my cordless telephone and it works just fine. Not as good as a permanent phone, but a good alternative.

____ *Typewriter.* If you have the skills.

____ *Typewriter correction fluid or paper.*

____ *Wastebasket.*

You now have an office space that can function to your maximum. This addition to your lifestyle should certainly make you more efficient in other areas of your life. It will give you a feeling of accomplishment.

Automobile

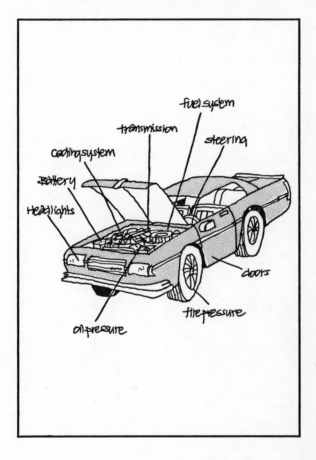

A Checklist for Your Car Before Taking a Trip

Stay away from any Christian who
spends his days in laziness and does
not follow the ideal of hard work.
—*2 Thessalonians 3:6*

*A*S IN ALL phases of life the three most important parts of any project are to PLAN, PLAN, PLAN. Usually things go wrong when we don't spend enough time in our planning phase. Don't be in such a hurry that you forget to plan. Plan to have your car regularly checked by a reliable mechanic and before starting off on that all-important trip. Many times we think of vacations only in the summer months, but depending upon your schedule flexibility you might well take your trip any time of the year.

Having your car checked regularly is the best way to prevent major car problems down the road when you are really counting on your car to perform properly. A combination of getting your car in shape and then paying close attention to the warning signals your car gives to you are key in assuring a car's smooth performance and longevity.

How do you know when your car needs attention? The Car Care Council gives some very practical suggestions.

1. Watch to see if your engine is hard to start, uses too much gas, seems sluggish, smokes, or is excessively noisy.

2. Be sure that your cooling and heating systems are in good condition. Be sure to check your hoses, belts, and anti-freeze/coolant.

3. How about those tires of yours? Heavy loads at high speeds are hard on tires. Make sure tires have plenty of tread and are properly inflated.

4. How's your oil? Oil is not only a lubricant, it is also a coolant. Clean, well-filtered oil will help your engine survive the heat as well as the cold.

5. Be sure to check your transmission. Does it slip when you shift gears? Is it noisy? Does it shift erratically? If you are towing a trailer, it is especially vital for your transmission to be in the best working order possible.

6. Be sure that the brakes stop evenly and are not making any strange noises.

7. Watch to see that all lights are working and that they are focused correctly. Also check turn signals and windshield wiper blades (for smearing or streaking).

After checking these areas of your car, you can feel more assured of a problem-free trip, barring unforeseen mechanical failure. If you do find yourself in car trouble in an unknown town and don't know of a good, reputable mechanic, you can look in the yellow pages under "Automotive Repairs" for ASE-certified technicians. These technicians have taken the proper courses to be certified by the National Institute for Automotive Service Excellence. This is an organization that is highly respected in the automotive industry, and is an independent, non-profit group which gives voluntary certification exams to technicians.

Pay Me Now
or Pay Me Later

An empty stable stays clean—
but there is no income from
an empty stable.

—Proverbs 14:4

*A*S CARS become more expensive it is to your advantage to keep a regular maintenance log on each of your cars. If you purchase a new car you will receive an owner's manual that will specify at what intervals you need to service your car and what maintenance is covered by your warranty. However, many people purchase older cars which are no longer covered by the new-car warranty.

As the old saying goes, "Pay me now or pay me later." You can either invest in preventative maintenance or pay more to repair breakdowns due to improper service on your automobile. A well-maintained car will bring greater driving pleasure; it will also be worth more when it is time to sell the older car to buy a newer model.

Place the following form (page 246, Figure 11) in a plastic divider in your glove compartment. Use one column each time the car is serviced. Your mechanic will tell you how often or how many miles you should service your car.

AUTOMOTIVE INFORMATION AND SERVICING SCHEDULE

Model _____

Serial # _____

Make _____

Insurance Company _____

License Number _____

Telephone # (___)_____

Use one column each time car is serviced	Date Mileage	Date Mileage	Date Mileage	Date Mileage	Date Mileage	Date Mileage	Date Mileage
Oil Change							
Lubrication							
Change oil Filter							
Clean Air Filter							
Service Cooling System							
Rotate Tires							
Replace Tires							
Service Brakes							
Plugs, Points, Condenser							
Engine Tune-up							
Change Trans. Fluid							
Total Cost	$	$	$	$	$	$	$

Figure 11

66

What to Do When Your Car Won't Start

Jehovah himself is caring for you!
He is your defender. He protects
you day and night.
—Psalm 121:5,6

*Y*OU'RE DRESSED in your finest Sunday clothes waiting for the family to join you in the car for church. You jump in your car, turn the key—and the car plays dead. If you've ever had that happen to you, you know the empty feeling you have.

The children arrive on the scene and of course ask 100 questions, which makes matters worse. What are you to do? Call a friend? A neighbor? A taxi? Or cancel the church service?

The American Automobile Association says failure of cars to start was the most common emergency last year.

Two ways a car can fail to start are 1) the starter motor may turn, but the engine refuses to catch, or 2) the starter motor may be sluggish, perhaps not turning at all.

Let's deal with the second case first.

If you twist the key and you hear only a click, at least you know the ignition switch works. If there was a click and your car has an automatic transmission, move the shift lever into neutral and then back to park and try starting the car again. Sometimes a little switch that prevents you from starting your car while it's in gear, sticks.

Still no start? See if the headlights light and the horn honks. If they seem weak, the battery is either dead or has a bad connection.

1. Find where the battery is—usually under the hood.

2. Look closely at the two terminals and the ends of the two cables, positive (+) and negative (–), that attach to them.

3. Are they clean and firmly secured?

4. If not, remove the negative (–) cable (it's usually black) *first*, followed by the positive (+) cable (usually red).

5. Scrape them with a knife or screwdriver and firmly reattach them.

If your car still won't start, you can either push-start it (but only if it has a stick shift) or jump-start it using cables attached to another car's battery. To push-start, you'll need:

1. A couple of strong children or neighbors, *or*

2. An experienced driver who is willing to give you a push from the rear of the car.

3. Get in the car; turn on the ignition.

4. Put your foot on the clutch and put the shift lever in second gear.

5. When the car reaches about 5 mph, let out the clutch and the car should start.

If you are attempting to jump-start your car, be sure to refer to the owner's manual. Great care should be taken when jump-starting your car.

After the car starts, drive to your mechanic's to check out why the battery was low and wouldn't start the engine. You may need a new battery or it may just need to be charged.

The second area to check if your starter turns, but the engine won't start, is the fuel or the ignition system. Be sure to check that you have gas in your tank!

If your car has fuel injection, you will probably want to have the car towed to your mechanic, because these are very hard to service by the average layman. But if it has a carbureted engine:

1. Pump the throttle pedal three times and try to start the car.

2. Still no response? Open the hood.

3. If you smell gas, you have flooded the carburetor.

4. Wait a few minutes.

5. Press the gas pedal all the way to the floor. Hold it there— *don't pump!*

6. The engine should sputter a bit and then start up.

Cold and damp weather present special challenges to a slumbering engine. On a cold day if the starter turns and if you have a carbureted engine:

1. Open the hood and find the air cleaner (usually big and round on top of engine, although sometimes rectangular).

2. Take off the wing nut or retaining clips and lift off the cover of the air cleaner.

3. Spray a little ether starter fluid (available at auto parts stores) down the carburetor throat.

Another useful elixir to carry in your trunk is WD-40; it absorbs moisture. On a damp day, spray some on the coil, some on the spark-plug wires and on the distributor, and some inside the distributor—if you can get the lid off. Then give the starter another turn.

If on a hot day your car refuses to start after it's been running, it may have a "vapor lock." If your car has a mechanical fuel pump (most carbureted engines do), pour cold water on the pump and nearby gas lines, and that should get you on your way.

If you don't have a very difficult problem, you should get to church in time to participate in the services. Try to relax and not get too uptight.

67

Car-Care Checklist

O Lord, you are worthy to receive
the glory and the honor and
the power, for you have
created all things.

—Revelation 4:11

*W*ITHOUT GIVING it a second thought, we jump into our car, turn the key in the ignition and expect our faithful buggy to start up and take us wherever we want to go.

But a car is an expensive piece of machinery, and, like our bodies, it needs care to run well. Being stuck with car trouble is no fun and can often be avoided.

Here is a checklist to help you keep your car in tiptop shape. It's especially important to give your car a checkup before going on a vacation or an extended trip.

Basic Checklist Before Taking a Trip

Don't be afraid to look over the service attendant's shoulder as he or she checks your car. You'll learn a great deal and can ask questions. Be sure the mechanic checks the following: engine oil level; coolant level (add only if below "add" mark); battery electrolyte level; windshield washer fluid level; and drive belt tension and condition.

Warning!

Do not remove the radiator cap quickly when the engine is hot, especially if the air conditioner has been used. Turn the cap slowly to let the steam escape. Otherwise you will be severely burned by hot water and steam.

Routine Maintenance Checklist

The following items need to be checked, especially before taking a long trip or vacation. Other than taking a trip, check these things twice a year. (The frequency of checkups depends somewhat on the type of climate you live in.)

If you take your car to a service station, don't assume that they automatically check these items. You'll need to ask for some of these services:

- Engine oil changed and filter replaced
- Air filter cleaned or replaced
- Emission control devices checked
- Headlights and brake lights inspected and adjusted
- Differential fluid level checked and changed (if applicable for your car)
- Transmission fluid level checked
- Wheel bearings inspected and repacked (once a year)
- Brakes inspected (once a year)
- Air-conditioning system checked and serviced once a year
- Cooling system hoses checked and coolant/antifreeze replaced once a year
- Power steering fluid level checked
- Shock absorbers tested
- Battery inspected
- Drive belts checked
- Windshield wipers. Even in summer you will need to replace if needed, in case of summer rainstorms.
- Tire tread depth and inflation pressure checked
- Exhaust system inspected for leaks
- Tune-up. Refer to owner's manual for manufacturer's suggestion for how often a tune-up is needed.

Emergency Organization List

These items should be carried in your car at all times in case of emergency:

- Fire extinguisher
- Jumper cables
- First-aid kit (bee-sting kit)
- Towel(s)
- Flashlight with extra batteries
- Ice scraper
- Spare fuses for electrical system
- Can of tire inflater/sealer
- Flares and/or highway triangular warning signs
- Spare drive belts, fan belts, air-conditioner belts, and air pump belts
- An empty approved gasoline container. *Do not carry extra gasoline in the trunk.*
- Container of water
- Warm blanket
- Metal or wire coat hanger
- Distress flag
- Plastic dropcloth for working under car
- Toolbox with the following: Pliers; screwdriver; adjustable wrench; small socket wrenches; hammer; cleanup wipes for hands; clean rag

Winter Tools

Chains, small shovel, can of sand, extra blankets or heavy coat for emergencies, heavy boots, and gloves.

It may seem overwhelming at first to furnish your car with these items, but it's well worth it. Being prepared could save a life or get you out of a dangerous or difficult situation. Besides, being ready for emergencies and keeping your car tuned up will relieve another whole area of stress in your life.

68

Automobile Organization— Travel Smart!

Love forgets mistakes; nagging about them parts the best of friends.

—Proverbs 17:9

*M*ANY WOMEN today are primarily responsible for their automobiles and need to know the basics of travel safety.

Be Prepared

Here is a helpful checklist of items to take with you in your car so you'll be prepared and ready to prevent minor roadside difficulties from becoming major ones.

Plan Ahead

Glove Compartment
- Maps
- Notepad and pen
- Tire-pressure gauge
- Cleanup wipes
- Sunglasses
- Mirror (best placed above sun visor)

- Extra pair of nylon hosiery for that unexpected run.
- Reading material, Bible—you can enjoy prayer and Bible reading during waiting times in the car.
- Can opener
- Plastic fork and spoon, for those yummy stops
- Change for phone calls
  Business cards
- Bandaids
- Matches
- Stationery—again, waiting can be used constructively to catch up on correspondence.
- Scissors, nail clippers
- Children's books and/or games

Trunk

(See "Emergency Organization List" on page 247–249 for car-care items that should be carried in case of emergencies.)

Protect Your Ownership

- Hide a key for the times you lock your keys inside the car. Caution: Don't put it under the hood if you have an inside hood-release.
- A good idea to prove ownership of your car is to print your name, address, and phone number on a 3 x 5 file card or use your business card and slide it down your car window-frame on the driver's side. If the car is lost or stolen, it is easier to prove the auto is yours.
- If you live in a potentially snowy area, keep a bag of kitty litter in your trunk. This will help give you traction if you are stuck in the snow.
- Your rubber carmats can be used to keep windshields from freezing. Put them on the outside of windows under your wipers to hold them in place, and presto . . . clean windows and no scraping either.
- Your car may not start if your battery terminals become corroded. Simply scrub them with a mixture of one cup of baking soda and two cups water. Presto! It cleans them right up.
- To remove decals and price lists from windows, simply sponge with plenty of white vinegar. Allow vinegar to soak in and stickers should come off easily.
- A rechargeable, battery-run, hand vacuum cleaner is very handy to have. It can be used to clean inside the car, carpet, and seats.

Time for You

Time for You–
Personal Grooming

Rejoice in the Lord, ye righteous;
and give thanks at the
remembrance of his holiness.
—*Psalm 97:12 KJV*

*T*HE OLD ADAGE "You only get one
time to make a first impression" is certainly true. We live in a time in history that stresses personal grooming. As Christians we need to keep moderation in mind and not be out of balance, but we must also be aware that we often conduct ourselves based on how we feel about our personal grooming. As I go shopping, I realize as I look at people that it takes so little to be above average. God wants us to be groomed properly as we go out into the secular world to be ambassadors for Him. Because how we look can affect our personal witness of who we are, I trust that some of these ideas will be helpful for your improved grooming.

Shampooing Your Hair

Lather hair twice only if very oily or very dirty. Otherwise you'll strip your hair of natural oils.

Don't be surprised if your favorite shampoo seems to leave your hair less bouncy after months of satisfactory performance. No one is exactly sure why but "shampoo fatigue" may be due to a buildup of proteins or other conditioning ingredients. Many people switch brands, only to perceive a drop in performance with the new shampoo within several months. At that point try switching back to the old one.

When you need a dry shampoo, try bran, dry oatmeal, baby powder, or cornstarch. Use a large-holed shaker or an empty baby-powder container to apply. Wash through hair with your fingers and brush out thoroughly.

Conditioning Your Hair

If you have an oily scalp, but dry or damaged hair, condition hair before you shampoo. Wet your hair, towel it dry, and then apply conditioner, starting an inch from your scalp. Work conditioner through your hair, wait five minutes, and rinse. Then shampoo as usual.

To revitalize and give luster to all types of hair: Beat three eggs; add two tablespoons olive or safflower oil and one teaspoon vinegar. Apply mixture to hair and cover with plastic cap. Wait half an hour and then shampoo well.

Here's a hair conditioner that is bound to draw raves! Combine 3/4 cup olive oil, 1/2 cup honey, and the juice of one lemon and set aside. Rinse hair with water and towel dry. Work in a small amount of conditioner (store leftovers in the refrigerator), comb to distribute evenly, and cover with a plastic cap for 30 minutes. Shampoo and rinse thoroughly.

When swimming daily in chlorinated or salt water, alternate hair care, using shampoo one day and conditioner the next.

Skin Products

A patch test for skin-care products: If you suspect you may be allergic to any substance, put a dab of it inside your wrist or elbow, cover it with an adhesive bandage, and leave it on for 24 hours. If no redness or irritation is evident, the product is probably safe. Because you can become allergic to something you have used regularly repeat this test whenever you haven't used a substance in several weeks and are concerned about a reaction from that product.

Change brands if you are experiencing a rash or lesions, or think you have an allergic reaction.

Cleansing Your Skin

To cleanse your face thoroughly, try the following method: Fill a clean sink with warm water, dip facial soap into the water, and rub the bar over your face. Dip the soap back into the water and make a lather in your hands. Massage this lather over your face. Rinse 15 to 20 times with the soapy water. Finish off with several cold-water rinses. Blot your face dry with a towel.

Excessive stinging or drying are signs that your toner, astringent, or aftershave lotion is too strong. Change brands or add one teaspoon of mineral water to each ounce of the product.

Hot weather tip: Refrigerator your facial toner, freshener, or astringent for a cool skin treat.

Bathing

In winter, your bath or shower water should be tepid—not hot, since hot water inflames the skin and increases moisture loss afterwards. Apply a moisturizing lotion right after bathing while your skin is still damp.

A simple but effective way to relieve dry skin and winter itch is to completely dissolve one cup of salt in a tub of water and bathe as usual. (For a more luxurious bath, try sea salt.) Bathing in salt often works better than using expensive bath oils, but if you really want to use oil, a plain mineral oil will generally fulfill your needs.

Moisturizing Your Skin

Always apply a moisturizer right after cleansing to prevent the surface moisture from evaporating. Moisturizers should last about ten hours. If your face feels tight before that time, freshen it with a toner and reapply your moisturizer. You may need a richer moisturizer.

Don't forget to moisturize your throat area. If this area is especially dry, heat peanut oil until warm and massage upward into your skin.

To avoid that cracked, flaky look on your elbows, make it a habit to pay special attention to them at the same time you lubricate the rest of your body.

If you have begun to get lines around your eyes and want to make them less obvious, rub eye cream between your fingertips to warm it before patting it around the eye area. This makes it easier for the skin to absorb the cream. Do not pull or stretch the skin around the eyes.

Sun Protection

Give your skin time to absorb a sunblock's ingredients before you need them. Apply sunscreen a half-hour before you go outdoors;

reapply after you swim or if you perspire heavily.

Take a long lunch hour away from outdoor exposure. The sun is highest in the sky and is most intense between the hours of 10:00 in the morning and 2:00 in the afternoon.

If you're planning on spending some time outdoors, use a moisturizing sunblock or sunscreen along with your regular moisturizer. Choose an SPF (sun protection factor) keyed to your skin's response to the sun. A fair person needs an SPF of 12 to 15.

Makeup Foundation

If you never seem to buy the right shade of foundation, try applying it just under the jawline rather than on the wrist. It should be just slightly lighter than your skin tone.

To transform a heavy, oil-based foundation into one that glides on more smoothly, add a bit of moisturizer or salt-free mineral water to the foundation. Use your palm or a small dish—not the makeup container—to do the mixing.

Blushers and Powders

For those "gray" days, mix a drop of liquid blusher with your foundation. Spread this instant glow all over your skin.

When you're feeling tired and dragged out, use blusher very lightly around the entire outer contour of your face, from the hairline to the chin, blending with a cosmetic sponge.

Under fluorescent lights, which destroy the rosy tones in the skin and give a yellowish look, apply your blusher a little darker and use a little deeper-colored lipstick.

Store loose powder in an old salt or pepper shaker so that you can shake it into your palm. Then dip a makeup brush or puff into the powder and dust it on.

Eye Makeup

Eye makeup is perishable. Bacteria from your eyes can be introduced to the product. Wash applicators frequently or use cotton swabs. Also, label shadows, pencils, and mascaras with their purchase dates. Replace your shadows and pencils every six months, your mascara every three months.

If you use liquid eyeliner, try dotting it on along the lash line. It will look less harsh than a solid line.

To get the sharpest point on your eyebrow, eyeliner, and lip pencils, put them in the freezer for an hour before sharpening.

Tame unruly eyebrows with a little bit of styling gel or mousse applied with an eyebrow brush.

Lip Care

Your lipstick will stay on much longer if you use the following method. Layer on in this order: face powder, lipstick, powder, lipstick. Wipe off excess powder with a damp washcloth or a tissue.

Remove Makeup

Never go to sleep without removing every trace of your makeup—except on your wedding night! Habitually sleeping with a layer of dirt, debris, and dead skin cells stuck to your face will leave your complexion looking muddy and dull.

When you're removing mascara, if it seems to get all over your face, wrap a tissue around your index finger and hold it just under the lower lashes. Remove eye makeup as usual with the other hand.

You are now well on your way of making that first good impression—may it wear well on you!

70

Organizing Your Prayer Time

> Be anxious for nothing, but in
> everything by prayer and
> supplication, with thanksgiving,
> let your requests be made known
> to God.
>
> —*Philippians 4:6 NKJV*

*D*URING MY early years of mother-
hood, I became frustrated about my
personal prayer time. I wanted to spend quality time with my Lord
but due to a busy schedule it just never worked out in a practical way.

One day through some trial and error I came up with a prayer
organization that worked for me. Here's what I did.

1. *Prayer Noteboook.* I purchased an inexpensive binder (5½ x
8½), one package of tabs, and one package of lined paper. The tabs
were labeled "Monday," "Tuesday," "Wednesday," etc. Next I
made a list of all things I wanted to pray for—family, finances,
church, missionaries, etc. I then delegated these requests into my
prayer notebook behind each tab. On Monday I now pray for each
member of the family. On Tuesday I pray for our church, the pastor,
the staff, etc. On Wednesday, I pray for people who are ill, and so on.
The Sunday tab is for sermon notes and outlines. I filter any prayer
requests into the weekly tabs so my prayer time does not overwhelm
me. I spend time reading my Bible, then I open my prayer notebook
to the tab for that day. I pray for the items behind that tab. The next

day I do the same, moving on through the next week.

   2. *Prayer Basket.* Try the following steps:

     a. Purchase a medium-size basket with a handle.

     b. Place in your basket your Bible, prayer notebook, a few postcards, a box of tissue, and a small bunch of silk flowers.

     c. Place your basket in an area you pass daily, perhaps on a table, the kitchen counter, your desk, or in the bathroom, etc.

     d. Schedule a daily time to spend time with your prayer basket in the morning, afternoon, or evening. Plan this time (five to 50 minutes) to pick up your basket and take it to a quiet place where you will use the ingredients during your prayer time.

     • The Bible—read God's Word daily.

     • Pray for the daily requests.

     • Write a short note to someone who needs encouragement on your postcards. Or you might simply say, "I prayed for you today." Some days I cry through my whole prayer time. My tissue is right there in my basket. The flowers give encouragement and lighten my heart as I look at God's creation.

My prayer basket is so personal and special to me. Some days I walk by my basket and it may be three o'clock in the afternoon. It says to me, "Emilie, you haven't picked me up today." What a reminder and what a challenge to my heart and spirit to pick up my prayer basket, putting it to use every day in spending special time with my Lord.

Proverbs 16:3 says, "Commit your works to the Lord, and your plans will be established" (NASB).

The days I pick up my prayer basket, my day, my life, and my organization as a busy woman go so much smoother. I have strength to meet the schedules and stresses that usually come.

71

New Year Organization

Oh, give thanks to the Lord, for he
is good; his love and his kindness
go on forever.
—1 Chronicles 16:34

*R*ECENTLY AFTER finishing a seminar on how to organize your household,
I talked to a young mother who said, "I loved all the organizational
ideas and tips you gave for the family and the home, but what about
me—my personal organization?" I gave her a copy of *My Daily
Planner*, a tool I have used for years to get me through each day,
week, month, and year of my life. Organization really does begin
with our own personal lives. Once we have ourselves organized, we
can move into the other areas of our lives such as our home or job.

Here are the tools you need to make your own daily planner. (If
you would rather purchase a premade planner, *My Daily Planner* is
published annually by Harvest House.)

• A small purse-size binder with paper
• Blank tabs you can label yourself
• A calendar

Label your tabs in the following way.

Tab 1: Goals

List long-range and short-range goals including daily, weekly, monthly, and yearly priorities. This will help you get your priorities in order. Include the following: Scriptures to read, prayer requests, priorities to accomplish, and family goals, as well as spiritual, household, work-related, financial, and budget goals.

Tab 2: Calendar

Purchase a small month-at-a-glance calendar at a stationery store and insert it into your binder. As you learn to write activities and commitments down, you will be surprised at how much less complicated your life becomes.

Tab 3: Daily Planner

In this section, list your daily appointments from morning to evening. This is not only useful for the mother who works outside her home but also for the homemaker who wants to get her daily household duties done in a more orderly manner.

Tab 4: To Do, To Buy

Make a note here of all the things you need to do when you have an errand day, such as:
- Pick up winter coat at the cleaners.
- Go to the grocery store for birthday candles.
- Take package to the post office.
- Buy vitamins at health food store.

Tab 5: Notes

Here is a place to write down notes from:
- Speakers and sermons
- Meetings and Bible studies
- Projects

Tab 6: Miscellaneous

Keep topical lists in this section such as:
- Emergency phone numbers
- Dentist/physician
- Babysitters' phone numbers

- Favorite restaurant phone numbers
- Books and music recommended

Tab 7: Expense Account

This section is especially for work-related expense outside the home.
- Who it was for and the amount and how it was paid for (cash, credit card, or check)
- What it was for: transportation, parking, food, promotion, or gas

Tab 8: Prayer Requests

Make colored insert tabs for each day of the week, Sunday through Saturday. Then write a comprehensive list of your prayer requests along with those of your friends and family, and divide them into five special lists. Assign each list to one day for one week, Monday through Friday. Leave Saturday as a swing day for immediate prayer requests.

Sunday's section should be left open for the pastor's sermon. That way you have a history of Scripture and content for later reference or study. If someone mentions a prayer request at church, you can assign it to a special day of the week when you get home.

In this way you can cover your prayer needs over a week's time. Date the request when you enter it into your book and then record the date when it is answered. Over a period of time you will have a history of how God has worked in your life. Remember, too, that not all prayers are immediately answered by "yes" or "no." Some are put "on hold" for awhile.

I'll guarantee that by implementing these few helpful ideas into your new year, you'll be on your way to the "organized you."

72

How to Organize Your Handbag

Keep alert and pray. Otherwise
temptation will overpower you. For
the spirit indeed is willing, but how
weak the body is!
—Matthew 26:41

*R*EMEMBER THE last time you rummaged through your handbag digging through old receipts, papers, tissue, half-used lipsticks, unwrapped Lifesavers, and that unmailed letter you thought was lost months ago? Handbags have a way of becoming catchalls, places where you have everything and can find nothing. You can get your handbag into top shape with just a little effort and organization. If you keep a well-organized handbag, it will be so simple to change bags and do it quickly.

Materials Needed

A nice-size handbag for everyday and three to seven small purses in various colors and sizes. (The small purses can be of quilted fabric, denim, or corduroy prints with zipper or velcro fasteners.)

How to Organize

1. *Wallet*
   Money/check book

    Change compartment
    Pen/credit cards
    Pictures (most-used)
    Driver's license
    Calendar (current)
2. *Makeup Bag 1*
    Lipstick
    Comb/small brush
    Blush
    Mirror
    Dime or quarter (phone change)
3. *Makeup Bag 2*
    Nail file
    Small perfume
    Hand cream
    Nail clippers
    Scissors (small)
    Tissues
    Breath mints/gum/cough drops
    Matches
4. *Eyeglass Case*
    For sunglasses
5. *Eyeglass Case*
    For reading/spare glasses
6. *Small Bag 1*
    Business cards—yours & your husband's, hair dresser, insur-
        ance agent, auto club, doctor, health plan
    Library card
    Seldom-used credit cards
    Small calculator
    Tea bag/artificial sweetener/aspirin
7. *Small Bag 2*
    Reading material—small Bible, paperback book
    Toothbrush
    Cleanup wipes
    Needle/thread/pins/thimble
    Band-Aid
    Toothpicks
    Tape measure
    Feminine protection

By taking some time to set it up you can organize your purse and avoid last minute frustration and stress.

73

Planning a Picnic for Happy Memories

Create in me a new, clean heart, O
God, filled with clean thoughts and
right desires.
—Psalm 51:10

*F*UN-FILLED memories of special family
times can happen by taking a picnic meal
to the park, lake, mountains, beach, desert, or favorite picnic area.

I was four years old when we took a picnic lunch to the desert
under a yucca tree. The setting doesn't sound real exciting but I can
still remember the green-and-white checkered tablecloth my mother
pulled out and spread on the ground, along with plates, glasses,
silver utensils, and delicious food. She took me by the hand and we
picked a few wild desert flowers for the table. Later we took a nature
walk and collected fun memories.

Picnics are for everyone and loved by everyone, and they can be
planned for any time of the year (though as the weather begins to
warm up, the creative picnics seem to warm up too). Early American
picnics were called "frolics" and consisted of games, music, flirta-
tions, and good food. Keep this in mind as you keep your American
picnics filled with the same ingredients.

You can plan themes around your region or other regions of our
country or even the world. Some ideas might be:

- A Vermont Snow Snack
- A New England Clam Bake
- A Hawaiian Luau
- An Abalone Steak Picnic
- A San Francisco Crab Lunch
- An Indian Summer Brunch
- Mexican Memories
- A Mardi Gras Feast
- A Pumpkin Patch Picnic

These themes are starting points to plan our food selections. Draw the family into this planning and research for what food you are going to take along for this special event. Don't make this just a mom's project—involve the whole family. The Mardi Gras feast might include chicken gumbo, steamed rice, marinated green beans, and New Orleans King Cake.

The pantry is a good source for the basic food selections. If you need to make a market run to purchase special items, do so at a time when the store is less crowded. Try early in the morning or late in the evening. Stay away from peak shopping hours.

Keeping Foods Cold

Once you have purchased and/or prepared your food, you need to plan how to keep your food cold. The length of time in which food can spoil is relative to the temperature outdoors, but it also depends upon the way the food was cooked, chilled, wrapped, and carried. Foods containing mayonnaise, eggs, cream, sour cream, yogurt, or fish are safe unrefrigerated up to two hours if the weather is fairly cool. If it will be more than two hours before you eat, plan to carry along a refrigerated cooler. Cool dishes as quickly as possible after preparing them and leave them in the refrigerator until just before time to leave. *Remember: Never take anything on a picnic that could possibly spoil unless you can provide effective portable refrigeration.*

There are a lot of excellent commercial coolers on the market. Select a size that will be adequate for your family's need. You can chill food in the cooler by using ice cubes, crushed or chipped ice, blocks from ice machines, or blocks frozen in clean milk cartons or other containers. Or you can fill plastic bottles (two-thirds full) with water to allow for expansion and freeze them overnight. These frozen containers eliminate the mess of melted ice.

Packing, Transporting, and Safe-Storing Tips

Prepare all food as close to departure time as comfortably possible for you. Don't cook in advance earlier than the time recommended in the recipe unless the item can be frozen successfully.

Try to pack your hamper or other carryall in reverse order from the way in which you'll use each item at the site. Place your food containers right-side-up to prevent spills and breakage.

Breakable glassware can be wrapped in the tablecloth, napkins, kitchen towels, or newspaper.

Foods such as pies, tarts, cakes, muffins, mousses, molded salads, or home-baked breads that crumble easily can be carried in the pans in which they were prepared. If the supplies do not fill the hamper, fill in with rolled newspaper or paper towels to prevent foods from overturning or bumping together.

Bags

Shopping bags are excellent for holding many items for a simple picnic. Use those fancy, attractive bags for transporting excess items that won't fit into the main picnic hamper. You might also want to carry along a large bag for your unwanted trash. Leave the site clean.

Ground Covers and Tablecloths

Choose a blanket, patchwork quilt, bedspread, sheet, comforter, afghan, or any large piece of fabric for a ground cover and tablecloth. Top it, if you like, with a decorative second cloth that fits the mood of the picnic you've planned.

No-iron cotton or synthetic fabric is easy to keep clean and ready for traveling. Other choices to consider are beach towels, bamboo or reed matting, nylon parachute fabric, flannel shirt material, or lengths of any easy-care fabric stitched at each end.

Purchase one or two plastic painters' drop cloths or carry a canvas tarpaulin to put down before you spread the tablecloth if the ground is damp, dusty, or snow-covered.

Baskets/Hampers

Wicker baskets or hampers are the traditional picnic carryalls. However, anything goes these days. Import shops sell baskets made in many different shapes, sizes, and price ranges.

The important thing is the time spent with your family and friends sharing your love together.

74

Beating
Jet Lag
in Travel

> Praise ye the Lord. O give thanks
> unto the Lord, for he is good, for
> his mercy endureth forever.
>
> —*Psalm 106:1*

*W*E LIVE in a fast-paced world of travel, and many times our body suffers as a result. We find ourselves unable to function as we should even though we have important business and social functions to perform.

As I travel throughout our continent I do certain things that help me minimize the effects of jet lag on my speaking schedule.

Jet lag is caused by rapid air travel over multiple time zones. The sudden change in time upsets synchronized body rhythms, resulting in physical and mental confusion. Research shows that the human body clock, set by stimuli like light and diet, can be "tricked" into adjusting to a new schedule. Here are some facts about jet lag and tips to avoid it.

Effects on the Body Clock

Many of our body cycles are affected by jet lag. We find rapid increases in our heartbeat, breathing, cell division, eye blinking, and swallowing. Our daily cycles of blood pressure, eyesight, mental ability, physical ability, sleep/wake rhythm, digestion, reproduction, temperature, metabolism, and sense of time are also disturbed.

Symptoms of Jet Lag

Some of the early signs of jet lag are fatigue, disorientation, reduced physical ability, reduced mental ability, upset appetite, and off-schedule bowel and urinary movements. Later symptoms of constipation or diarrhea, insomnia, acute fatigue, loss of appetite, headaches, lack of sexual interest, and slowed response-time to visual stimulation are also negative side effects.

Fighting Off Jet Lag

• *Diet*. Eating certain foods helps adjust the body clock. Foods high in carbohydrates induce sleep; those high in protein produce wakefulness. On a typical seven-hour flight over several time zones, you might try the following schedule to help reduce jet lag.

• *Three days before flight*. Eat a high-protein breakfast and lunch, a high-carbohydrate dinner, and caffeinated drinks (if ʼou use) between 3:00 P.M. and 4:30 P.M. only.

• *Day of flight*. Get up earlier than usual, eat a high protein breakfast and lunch, a high-carbohydrate dinner, and shortly after 6:00 P.M., drink two to three cups of black coffee. Reset watch to destination time.

• *During flight, day of arrival*. Don't oversleep. A half-hour before breakfast (destination time) activate your body and brain, eat a high-protein breakfast and lunch, a high-carbohydrate dinner, drink, no caffeine, avoid napping, and go to sleep at 10:00 P.M. (destination time).

• *Consult an aircraft seating chart*. Request bulkhead or emergency exit seats, which have more leg room.

• *Don't drink alcohol*. It causes dehydration. Drink water.

• *Sleep and eat on your destination time schedule*. Ask the flight attendant to serve your meals at your specified time.

• *Avoid big meals*. Air pressure causes gas in the intestines to expand.

• *Request a special meal*. Do this 24 hours in advance from the airline if needed.

• *Don't wear contact lenses*. On long flights, they dry out.

• *Bring a game or book*. This will provide mental stimulation.

• *Don't cross your legs*. This interferes with blood circulation.

Tips to Start and Organize a Home Business

> She considers a field and
> buys it; out of her earnings
> she plants a vineyard.
> —*Proverbs 31:16* NKJV

*T*ODAY'S WOMAN approaches the 1990's with much excitement. We've come a long way, women. The 80's found us making a lot of changes from home to work, with accompanying stress, frustration, disorganization, and fatigue. For some of us, our priorities went out the window along with our organized homes and meals. We gave up our children to babysitters and daycare and our meals to fast-food stores. Our spiritual life moved into low gear— not for everyone, but for many. However, new changes are coming into focus. We are tired of the tired 80's. More women are feeling the desire to be at-home mothers and career women. That's exciting. We are beginning to see the working woman find balance between work and home, with a new interest in home business (85 percent of new businesses are started by women in their homes). Many women will make a personal choice to be at home in the 90's, while many will continue jobs outside due to need or desire.

My mother became a single working parent when my father died. I was 11 years old. She opened a small dress shop and we lived in the back in a small, three-room apartment. Home and career were mixed. Mom not only sold clothing but worked late into the night doing alterations. Bookkeeping was also done after hours. We survived because we all helped in a time of need. When our children were small I developed a small business out of our home; the extra money was for extra things. I was able to do that because I felt somewhat organized and in control of our home.

This may very well be the year God will bring into your life the desire to be an at-home woman and develop a from-home business. Yes, to be successful it does take time, creativity, balance and desire. Our ministry, "More Hours In My Day," began in our home and has stayed there for over nine years. Books have been written, seminars given, and mail orders sent from our door to many of yours.

Our typist, Sheri, runs a typing service from her home and is enjoying better profits than ever before. A dear and longtime friend, Rose, has a small business called "Tiffany Touch" where she goes into other people's homes in her area and does everything from organizing drawers to hanging pictures. A mother with a new baby designed a slip-over-the-head bib that is sold all over the country out of her home. Still another mom created designer baby bottles—she changed baby diapers into cash of over $1 million.

Connie Lund, out of Olympia, Washington created a small devotional flip chart of inspiration called "Reaching Up to God" and through their sales is sending her daughter through college. When her daughter comes home for vacations she helps collate and tie the charts. Most at-home businesses develop family oneness, with everyone working together to help one another.

Direct sales are popular and profitable. Tupperware, Avon, Shaklee, Amway, Mary Kay, Home Interiors, Christmas Around the World, Successful Living Books, Choice Books—from home parties to door-to-door, these are just a few.

One woman I read about shops for working women, buying groceries and gifts, and running errands from picking up dry cleaning to buying stamps at the post office. She even delivered a lunch to a schoolchild who forgot it at home.

Another creative mom started gift wrapping for people (men in offices), which led to food baskets and then homemade wreaths and flower arrangements.

Another mom advertised her famous chili recipe for $1—and sold enough to buy Christmas presents for the whole family. She was very pleased and surprised. Aimee made colorful earrings. Women saw them on her and wanted a pair for themselves. From friends to boutique shops, sales multiplied.

All kinds of arts and crafts have created many added funds for the family income.

I was visiting some friends who received an adorable loaf of bread shaped like a teddy bear, a novelty gift that is now being shipped all over the state.

Nancy is a single parent who quit her computer job and started her own service in her home. She is able to be home with her three children and still run a very successful business.

Nancy and Elizabeth teamed up and are designing and selling Christian greeting cards, business cards, and Christmas cards, and are doing very well.

Some women are working at home as employees—sales reps, technical service reps, claim adjusters, and many others who are unsalaried employees but who spend most of their time in the field. Their employers typically don't provide an office so their files, desk phone, etc. are in their homes. Many other women could do part-time employment in the same way. Naturally you have to ask yourself if you have the space in your home for such types of employment.

I have a friend who represents designer clothing out of her home four times a year. She sends out invitations with days and hours, then books appointments and helps the women coordinate their wardrobes.

The 90's woman, I believe, will get back to home shopping and parties from jewelry to clothing to household products.

As we move further this year, set your desires high and chart out your goals for your future this year. Where would you like to be next year at this time? What will you need to accomplish to get there?

When can you start? Possibly now. 1) Your desire is to be working from home—by next year. 2) Make calls and talk with friends, family, and business associates. 3) Perhaps you need to take a class on business, sales, design, etc.

Many of you may be happy just working where you are. Others may want to cut hours to be at home a little more. Whatever you want to accomplish this year you can do with a positive attitude, desire, and creativity wrapped with prayer.

My desire is to see the busy woman get back to traditional values and to use her God-given creativity wherever she may be—in or out of the home. Changes will come in the future as they have in the past, but yours can come with a positive outlook and priorities of God, family, and career.

The following are some ideas and tips on how to implement or begin a business at home.

Research

1. Find others who are in your same field of home business and talk with them. They can provide a wealth of information.
2. Will it benefit you to advertise in your local telephone book?
3. What kind of advertising should you use other than word of mouth?

Goals

1. Determine a time schedule to be at home with your business. Example: Within one year.
2. Sign up for a class at your local community college on simple business bookeeping.

Finances

1. Draw up a projected budget for yourself. What will be your credits, your debits? How much money do you need to launch your business?
2. Consider the costs involved in advertising.
3. Set aside some money for start-up expenses and supplies such as a typewriter, copy machine, furniture, and for small desk-top items, such as stapler, scissors, etc.
4. Start writing down hidden costs. There will always be expenses that you did not count on so the more research you do the less likely you will be to have a lot of surprises.

Home Preparation

1. What area will you use and how much space do you need?
2. Can you use your same phone system?
3. Do you need a desk, work tables, file cabinets, etc.?
4. Will any carpentry work be required?

Legalities

1. Get information on what legal matters need to be considered. Some home businesses will require a business license. Check with your local county records department.
2. Obtain a resale number if needed.
3. What kind of deductions are you eligible for? It is advisable to contact a CPA who is knowledgeable in the field of home business deductions.

Hours

1. Think through how many hours you will reasonably be able to work per day, per week, per month.
2. Will you need to work around children's schedules?
3. Will you have regular business hours?
4. When will you clean your home, cook meals, etc.?
5. Don't forget you—schedule time to do a few things for yourself, such as hair appointments, shopping, church, friends, Bible studies, etc.

Like many situations, there will be a lot of trial and error. You'll learn much as you grow along, and the benefits will be great!

Miscellaneous

27 Things to Help You Survive an Earthquake

We are hard-pressed on every side,
yet not crushed.
—*2 Corinthians 4:8 NKJV*

*I*N CALIFORNIA we are always concerned about the earth moving. Animals
often hear the rumble of the earth before their owners sense that
something is about to happen. It is truly an experience that a person
will never forget—his or her first earthquake and every one thereaf-
ter.

If you live in California or some other earthquake-prone area, or
are planning to visit such an area for business or pleasure, you may
want to become familiar with the following recommendations as
suggested by the American Red Cross.

Basics to Do During an Earthquake

1. Stay CALM.
2. *Inside:* Stand in a doorway, or crouch under a desk or table,
   away from windows or glass dividers.
3. *Outside:* Stand away from buildings, trees, and telephone and
   electric lines.

4. *On the Road:* Drive away from underpasses, overpasses; stop in safe area; stay in vehicle.

Basics to Do After an Earthquake

1. Check for injuries—provide first aid.
2. Check for safety—check for gas, water, and sewage breaks; check for downed electric lines and shorts; turn off appropriate utilities; check for building damage and potential safety problems during aftershocks, such as cracks around chimney and foundation.
3. Clean up dangerous spills.
4. Wear shoes.
5. Turn on radio and listen for instructions from public safety agencies.
6. Use the telephone only in emergency situations.

Basic Survival Items to Keep on Hand

1. Portable radio with extra batteries.
2. Flashlight with extra batteries.
3. First-aid kit, including specified medicines needed for members of your household.
4. First-aid book.
5. Fire extinguisher.
6. Adjustable wrench for turning off gas and water.
7. Smoke detectors properly installed.
8. Portable fire escape ladder for homes and apartments with multiple floors.
9. Bottled water sufficient for the number of members in your household for a week.
10. Canned and dried foods sufficient for a week for each member of your household. *Note:* Both water and food should be rotated into normal meals of household so as to keep freshness. Canned goods have a normal shelf-life of one year for maximum freshness.
11. Nonelectrical can opener.
12. Portable stove such as butane or charcoal. *Note:* Use of such stoves should not take place until it is determined that there is no gas leak in the area. Charcoal should be burned only out of doors. Use of charcoal indoors will lead to carbon monoxide poisoning.
13. Several dozen candles. The same caution should be taken as in the above note on portable stoves.

14. Matches.
15. Telephone numbers of police, fire, and doctor.

Basics You Need to Know

1. How to turn off gas, water, and electricity.
2. Basic first aid.
3. Plan for reuniting your family.

As with any emergency program that you have for your family, you must review it every three months to make sure the members of your family know what to do in case of an earthquake. The plan for evacuating the home and the plan for reuniting the family if the various members of the family are away from home should be walked through so the instructions are thoroughly understood by all members of the family.

Remember,

THE BEST SURVIVAL
IS A PREPARED SURVIVAL!

Record-Keeping
Made Simple

> No one can become my disciple
> unless he first sits down and counts
> his blessings—and then renounces
> them all for me.
>
> —*Luke 14:33*

*T*HIS IS THE YEAR to get our records,
bills, and receipts out of shoeboxes,
closets, drawers, and old envelopes. I found that I could clean out my
wardrobe closet fairly easily. I could toss an old skirt, stained blouse,
or a misfit jacket with little difficulty; however, where and when I
should toss old financial records was very difficult. I didn't want to
do the wrong thing, so I kept saving—usually too long.

At income-tax time my neck always got stiff because I knew Bob
was going to ask for a canceled check or a paid invoice and I wasn't
sure if I had it or not. At that point, I made a decision to get my
record-keeping in order so that it was a very easy process to keep my
records up-to-date.

I sat down and looked at the whole process of record-keeping and
began to break it down into logical steps. My first step was to decide
to keep my records. Since I like things to be in order with the
minimum amount of paperwork, I had a tendency to throw away
records that should have been saved. I found that throwing away
Bob's salary stubs, last year's tax return, or current receipts for

medical or business expenses would only bring problems further down the road.

Our CPA says that throwing away financial records is the biggest mistake that people make. Throwing away records that later turn out to be important causes people a lot of unnecessary work and worry, he cautioned. When you have an IRS audit and you can't prove your deductions by a canceled check, or a paid invoice, you will lose that deduction for that year, and be subject to a fine and interest due as well. Records are very important.

Good financial records help you make decisions very quickly. In just a few moments you can retrieve valuable information so that a decision can be made for budget planning, future purchases, or just anticipated future income.

As I began to develop a plan to establish good record-keeping, I came up with a seven-step program.

STEP 1: Know what to keep

I discovered that records generally fall into two categories: PERMANENT records (important to keep throughout your life) and TRANSITORY records (dealing with your current circumstances).

Permanent records would include personal documents required in applying for credit, qualifying for a job, or proving entitlement to Social Security and other government programs. Birth and marriage certificates, Social Security cards, property records, college transcripts, diplomas, and licenses all fall into this category.

Deciding how long to retain transitory records can be more difficult because often you don't know how long you'll need them. As a rule of thumb I suggest you keep all employment records until you leave the job. Other transitory records you want to keep include receipts for any major purchases you have made—jewelry, autos, art—stock certificates, tax returns and receipts (for at least six years), health insurance policies, credit union membership and company stock ownership plans. Canceled checks not relating directly to specifics like home improvements should be kept for a minimum of three years in case of a tax audit; however, I will usually keep them five to six years just to make sure I'm not throwing any records away that I might need on a tax audit.

If you own your home, apartment, or mobile home, be sure to retain the receipts for any improvements you make until you sell the property. They become proof that you added to the property's value and will reduce any capital gains you might owe. Don't discard these receipts or tax returns from the year in which you paid for the improvements. I usually make a copy of this kind of receipt and keep a permanent copy in my "Home" folder. I have found that this saves a lot of valuable time when I need to justify each record. In my "Home" folder I also keep a running log with date, improvement made, cost, and receipt for each expenditure. At any given time we know how much money we have invested in our home. This information really helps when you get ready to sell your home and you want to establish a sales price.

Your tax return, wage statements, and other papers supporting your income and deductions should be kept at least six years (that's the IRS statute of limitations for examining your return). However, you will need to keep real estate and investment records longer if you will need to verify purchase prices in the future. I retain our records for six years, because the IRS has the right to audit within six years if they believe you omitted an item accounting for more than 25 percent of your reported income, or indefinitely if they believe you committed fraud.

STEP 2: Know yourself when you set up your system

Try to keep your system as simple as you can. I have found that the more disorganized you are, the simpler the system should be. It doesn't make sense to set up an elaborate filing system if it is too complicated for you to follow.

I suggest that you consider these points when setting up your system:
- How much time can you devote to record-keeping? The less time you have, the simpler your system should be.
- Do you like working with numbers? Are you good at math? If so, your system can be more complex.
- How familiar are you with tax deductions and financial planning? If you are a beginner, set up a simple system.
- Will anyone else be contributing records to the system?

This last point is a very important consideration if you are married. Mates may have a different opinion on what type of system you should have. I have found among married couples that it usually works best when you determine who is most gifted in this area and let that person take care of the records. Bob and I get along very well in this area. I write the checks for our home expenses and balance this account's checking statement. Then I forward the material to Bob for record-keeping. In our family he is the most gifted in this area of our life.

We have found that the simplest way to organize receipts for tax purposes is to keep two file folders, one for deduction items and another for questionable items. At tax time all you have to do is total up each category and fill in the blank. Be sure to double-check the other entries for overlooked possibilities.

If your return is more complex, set up a system with individual folders for the various deductions you claim: medical and dental expenses, business, travel, entertainment, property taxes, interest on loans, childcare services. When you pay a bill, drop the receipt into the right folder. At the end of the year, you'll be able to tally the receipts and be set to enter the totals on your tax forms.

Be sure to take your questionable-deduction folder with you when you go to see your CPA. Go over each item to see if it is eligible for a deduction. As you can tell by reading this chapter, I strongly endorse using a professional tax-preparer. Tax returns have become so difficult and the tax laws so complex that good stewardship of your money may require that you go to a professional. Tax-preparers will save you much more than you will spend for their services.

Your checkbook can be your best record-keeper if you check off entries that might count as tax deductions. If you have a personal computer at home, you have a wide selection of software programs to help you keep track of these records.

STEP 3: Set aside a spot for your records

Generally, home rather than office is the best place for personal documents. A fireproof, waterproof file cabinet or desk drawer is excellent for transitory records. However, I use and have thousands of other ladies all across the United States using our Perfect Boxes to store records.

Permanent documents generally should be kept in a safe-deposit box However, your will and important final instructions should be kept in a different place because in many states, safe-deposit boxes are sealed following the owner's death, even if someone else has a key.

STEP 4: Tell someone where your records are

As I travel around the country conducting seminars, many of the ladies tell me they don't know where their husbands have anything written down in case of death. None of us like to think about death because it is so far away, but we must share this important information with those people who will need to know.

Each year Bob reviews with me his "data sheet" listing all the information regarding insurance policies, stocks and investments, mortgage locations, banking account information, contents in safe-deposit boxes, etc. That information is very helpful and reassuring to me in case of any changes in our status.

Even if you're a whiz at keeping financial records, the records are not very useful if no one else knows where any of them are located. As a family, make up a list noting where your records are located and give it to a family member or trusted friend.

STEP 5: Get professional advice on handling records

As I've shared previously in this chapter, Bob and I recommend that you seek professional advice on how better records can translate into tax savings in the future. The expense is well worth the investment of time and money. You can also go to your local bookstore and purchase any number of good paperback books on this topic. Be a reader and a learner. It will serve you well.

STEP 6: Change your record-keeping system when you make a life change

Major life shifts—a job move, marriage, death, divorce, separation—signal a time to revamp your records. Starting a home-based business also means it's time to talk to the professional regarding new tax allowances. A life change usually necessitates a change in record-keeping.

The costs of looking for a new job in the same field and a job-related move can mean you're eligible for a new tax deduction, so be sure to file all receipts.

STEP 7: Set aside time for your record-keeping

Try to set a regular time each month to go over your financial records so that you won't be a wreck come April when you have to file your tax return. The best system in the world won't work if you don't use it or keep it current.

Many people prefer to update records when they pay bills. Others file receipts, update a ledger of expenses, and look over permanent records once a month when reconciling a checking account. Whatever works best for you is what's important. You should update at least once a month. If not, you will create a lot of stress playing catch-up. The goal of simple record-keeping is to reduce stress in our lives, not to increase the stress.

I have found that time is worth money. When I can reduce time, I can increase money because my energy is better spent on constructive efforts rather than always dealing with emergencies and putting out fires.

Home Fire Safety Survey

I will bless the Lord and not forget
the glorious things he does for me.

—*Psalm 103:2*

*A*FTER SPEAKING at a seminar one evening, a lovely woman shared with me her story of how a simple grease fire in the kitchen burned down her whole house. I had given a hint about using baking soda to put out kitchen fires, and about keeping a coffee can filled with baking soda close at hand by the stove. She said until that night she had never heard of that. I was totally surprised because I grew up knowing to use baking soda in case of household fires. Because of her story, I thought we needed to alert all homemakers to home fire safety. Many city and town fire departments will provide free inspections to help you identify any fire hazards in your home or business. Just give them a call and ask their help. Here is a fire safety survey for you who would like to do it yourself. It very well could save a life or the life of your home.

DO-IT-YOURSELF
HOME FIRE SAFETY SURVEY

Kitchen

YES / NO

- Are stove and vent clean of grease buildup? —— ——
- Are curtains or towel racks close to the stove? —— ——
- Are flammable liquids (cleaning fluids, etc.) —— ——
  stored near a heat source? Remember, even
  a pilot light can set vapors on fire.
- Is baking soda close at hand? —— ——

Bedrooms

- Are smoke detectors installed and tested monthly? —— ——
- Are there two ways out of the room? —— ——
- If the bedroom is on the second floor, is there —— ——
  an escape ladder by the window?

Halls and Stairways

- Are smoke detectors installed and tested monthly? —— ——

Living and Dining Rooms

- Is there insufficient air space around TV and —— ——
  stereo that could cause them to overheat?
- Are curtains, furniture, or papers near a space —— ——
  heater? (Kerosene heaters are not allowed in
  living quarters.)
- Is there a spark screen on the fireplace? —— ——

Garage

- Are gasoline, paint thinners, and/or other flam- —— ——
  mable liquids stored in a ventilated area away
  from open flames? (hot water heater, furnace)
- Are flammable liquids stored in an approved —— ——
  safety container?
- Is the hot water heater clear of any storage —— ——
  within 18 inches?
- Is the furnace clear of any storage within 18 —— ——
  inches and are filters changed on a regular basis?

- Is there a fire extinguisher nearby? —— ——
- Are oil-soaked rags stored in a covered metal —— ——
    container?

Outside

- Are house numbers visible from the street? —— ——
- Are numbers painted on curb? —— ——
- Are front and rear yards clear of debris? —— ——
- Are trees well-trimmed? —— ——
- Is the chimney spark arrester in place? —— ——

General

- Are multiplug adapters used with appliances? —— ——
- Are electrical cords in good condition? —— ——
- Are there overloaded outlets or extension cords? —— ——
- Are any extension cords run under rugs or —— ——
    carpets or looped over nails or other sharp
    objects that could cause them to fray? (The
    fire department discourages the use of
    extension cords. However, if using portable
    or temporary extension cords, check listing
    label on both cord and appliance to
    determine appropriate size and configuration
    of extension cord needed.)
- Are matches and lighters out of reach of young —— ——
    children?
- Has an emergency exit been planned, —— ——
    developed, and practiced?
- Is clothes dryer free of lint? —— ——
- Is firewood or lumber stored no less than ten —— ——
    feet from house?
- Is the 9-1-1 emergency number on or by phone? —— ——

These safeguards cannot guarantee you will not have a fire, but they will reduce the chances of a fire starting or spreading.

79

House-Hunting
Checklist

Lovest thou me more than these?
—John 21:15 KJV

$\mathscr{B}$UYING OR RENTING a house, apartment, condo (or tent!) can sometimes
be a source of stress. By midsummer, the anxiety of being settled
before school starts can cause you to make the wrong decisions when
house hunting in a hurry.

The checklist (page 293, Figure 12) will be helpful in keeping
track of the special features of the homes that you've seen. Use it to
compare them and single out that special house you want to make
your home.

This organized shopping list can be kept and copies made. It will
enable you to look back and compare!

If you have a Polaroid camera, take a picture of each home and
attach it to the back of each checklist form.

This type of organization will certainly give you more credibility
with the realtor and home-seller. They both will give you the benefit
of being a wise buyer.

HOUSE HUNT RECORD

Date _____

Address of home _____ Age _____

Best route to take _____

Owner of Home _____ Phone # _____

Salesperson _____

House design _____

House color _____

No. of square feet _____ Size of lot _____

Asking price _____ Down payment $ _____

Monthly payment $ _____

Type of utilities _____ Cost per month $ _____

Other costs _____

Garage? ☐ 1 Car ☐ 2Car ☐ Larger ☐ Carport

Condition/type of roof _____

Living room: Size _____ Flooring _____

Kitchen: Size _____ Flooring _____

Dining room: Size _____ Flooring _____

Storage space: Adequate? ☐ Yes ☐ No

Husband's first impression _____

Bedrooms: Number _____ Sizes _____

Bathrooms: Number _____ Sizes _____ Colors _____

Fixtures and tile condition _____

Water pressure check _____

Family room: Size _____ Flooring _____

Foyer: Size _____ Closet space _____

Game room: Size _____ Flooring _____

Basement: Size _____ ☐ Finished ☐ Unfinished

Laundry room: Size _____ Flooring _____

Other _____

☐ Central Air ☐ Fireplace Location(s) _____

Overall interior condition _____

☐ Patio ☐ Pool ☐ Pantry _____

Distance from work: Miles _____ Time _____

Distance from shopping: Miles _____ Time _____

Neighborhood rating _____

Overall rating of home and property _____

Schools: Quality _____ Distance from home _____

Comments _____

Wife's first impression _____

Figure 12

80

Pool Owner's Checklist– Safety First

> Happy are thy men, and happy are
> these thy servants, which stand
> continually before thee, and hear
> thy wisdom.
>
> —*2 Chronicles 9:7 KJV*

*A*S MORE AND more homes, apartments, condominiums, and mobile home parks offer swimming facilities of all types—above-ground pools, spas, vinyl lining, and conventional gunite pools— we must become more conscious of safety around water. Since there are so many opportunities to go swimming, we can't let down our alertness when we supervise our youngsters.

Nothing is more tragic than to lose a child to drowning or to a life of brain damage because we became complacent with water and its many dangers.

One scenario of a drowning might go like this: A three-year-old child is at home with one parent. A door to the swimming pool is unlocked. There is a fence around the yard per city code, but there is no interior fence around the pool. An outsider can't get to the pool easily, but the child at home is in trouble because he can get to the pool with no problem.

Mom answers the phone or goes to the bathroom. Supervision is interrupted for a minute or two. The child spots a plastic ball at the pool edge and quickly goes out the unlocked door and falls into the water trying to get the ball.

You may think it can't happen to you and your child, but many fire department personnel can give witness that it only takes one or two unattended moments.

Here is a pool safety checklist:

- Never leave a child alone near or in a pool or bathtub. Your quick phone call or trip to another part of the house leaves plenty of time for your unattended child to fall into the pool or tub.
- Give your child swimming lessons. (However, lessons don't replace constant supervision.)
- Call the local Red Cross chapter and enroll in a CPR class.
- Build a fence around all sides of the pool. Use nonclimbable material so the children can't climb over. Be sure to have a self-closing, self-latching gate. Fence should be at least four to five feet high.
- Doors leading to the pool should always be locked. Locks should be out of a child's reach. Kids can crawl through pet doors too.
- If a child can't swim he or she should not be allowed to dive head first into water, play on floats, play on inner tubes unattached to their bodies, or hold onto other children while in the water.
- Don't rely on flotation devices for protection.
- Consider door or floating pool alarms.
- Consider keeping a vinyl cover on your pool when it's not in use.
- Tell your babysitters or other guardians about drowning precautions. Encourage your babysitters to know CPR.
- Keep toys away from the pool. They are too tempting.
- Have a poolside phone with emergency telephone numbers.
- Have a long pole with a hook on it next to the pool so you could extend it to a child who might need some assistance.
- Do you know how to swim? If not, take lessons so you will personally feel confident around water.
- Spas, bathtubs, ponds, lakes, beaches, and toilets are potential drowning pools too.
- Purchase a long extension or cordless phone to take with you into the bathroom. Don't be tempted to leave your child unattended while in the tub.

SAFETY AROUND CHILDREN EXTENDS LIFE!

See *Survival For Busy Women*, also published by Harvest House, for many samples of useful charts.

"MORE HOURS IN MY DAY" can provide many of the organizational materials that are recommended in this book and others written by Emilie Barnes. You may obtain a price list and seminar information by sending your request and a stamped, self-addressed business envelope to:

MORE HOURS IN MY DAY
2838 Rumsey Drive
Riverside, California 92506

Other Good Harvest House Reading

MORE HOURS IN MY DAY
by *Emilie Barnes*

There can be more hours in your day when you use the collection of calendars, charts, and guides in this useful book on home time management.

THINGS HAPPEN WHEN WOMEN CARE
by *Emilie Barnes*

Things Happen When Women Care shows you how to carve out time for others by streamlining the details of daily living and home organization. This warm, insightful look at developing friendships and enlarging the boundaries of your personal ministry will give you the tools you need to start today on the great adventure of caring for others.

THE COMPLETE HOLIDAY ORGANIZER
by *Emilie Barnes*

The busy woman's answer to holiday planning, *The Complete Holiday Organizer* gives ideas and helpful hints to make celebration preparations easier. A brief history about each holiday will challenge you to begin your own family traditions.

THE SPIRIT OF LOVELINESS
by *Emilie Barnes*

Join Emilie Barnes as she shares insights into the inner qualities of spiritual beauty and explores the places of the heart where true femininity is born. With hundreds of "lovely" ideas to help you personalize your home, Emilie shows that beauty *can* be achieved with even the lightest touch of creativity. Your spirit of loveliness will shine through as you make your home a place of prayer, peace, and pleasure for your family.

EATING RIGHT!
by *Emilie Barne* and *Sue Gregg*

Bestselling author Emilie Barnes and Sue Gregg approach the conflicts involved in food selection, preparation, and kitchen organization with practical help and a *realistic* approach based on common-sense guidelines and God's plan for healthy eating.

SURVIVAL FOR BUSY WOMEN
Establishing Efficient Home Management
by *Emilie Barnes*

A hands-on manual for establishing a more efficient home-management program. Over 25 charts and forms can be personalized to help you organize your home.

THE CREATIVE HOME ORGANIZER
by *Emilie Barnes*

Bursting with fast and easy methods to save time and energy in your home, *The Creative Home Organizer* has helpful hints for every area of your home. You can learn how to manage a household economically and have fun while doing it!

THE WORKING MOTHER'S GUIDE TO SANITY
by *Elsa Houtz*

Working mothers "have it all"—or do they? *The Working Mother's Guide to Sanity* examines the most fundamental concerns and problems working mothers face. Elsa Houtz shows the sometimes-funny, sometimes-trying, and always challenging life of today's working mother.

WORKING AT HOME
by *Lindsey O'Connor*

Home businesses are sprouting up all over the country as more and more people are finding a way to combine parenting and working without having to give up traditional family roles. In *Working at Home*, Lindsey O'Connor helps you determine whether a home business is for you and how you can get one off the ground.

Dear Reader:

We would appreciate hearing from you regarding this Harvest House nonfiction book. It will enable us to continue to give you the best in Christian publishing.

1. What most influenced you to purchase *The 15-Minute Organizer*?
   - ☐ Author
   - ☐ Subject matter
   - ☐ Backcover copy
   - ☐ Recommendations
   - ☐ Cover/Title
   - ☐ _____

2. Where did you purchase this book?
   - ☐ Christian bookstore
   - ☐ General bookstore
   - ☐ Department store
   - ☐ Grocery store
   - ☐ Other

3. Your overall rating of this book:
   - ☐ Excellent   ☐ Very good   ☐ Good   ☐ Fair   ☐ Poor

4. How likely would you be to purchase other books by this author?
   - ☐ Very likely
   - ☐ Somewhat likely
   - ☐ Not very likely
   - ☐ Not at all

5. What types of books most interest you?
   (check all that apply)
   - ☐ Women's Books
   - ☐ Marriage Books
   - ☐ Current Issues
   - ☐ Self Help/Psychology
   - ☐ Bible Studies
   - ☐ Fiction
   - ☐ Biographies
   - ☐ Children's Books
   - ☐ Youth Books
   - ☐ Other _____

6. Please check the box next to your age group.
   - ☐ Under 18
   - ☐ 18-24
   - ☐ 25-34
   - ☐ 35-44
   - ☐ 45-54
   - ☐ 55 and over

Mail to: Editorial Director
Harvest House Publishers
1075 Arrowsmith
Eugene, OR 97402

Name _____

Address _____

City _____ State _____ Zip _____

Thank you for helping us to help you in future publications!